GUNS&AMMO
Guide to
SNIPING

GUNS&AMMO

Guide to
SNIPING

A COMPREHENSIVE GUIDE TO
GUNS, GEAR, AND SKILLS

EDITORS OF GUNS & AMMO

Skyhorse Publishing

Skyhorse Publishing books may be purchased in bulk at special discounts for sales promotion, corporate gifts, fund-raising, or educational purposes. Special editions can also be created to specifications. For details, contact the Special Sales Department, Skyhorse Publishing, 307 West 36th Street, 11th Floor, New York, NY 10018 or info@skyhorsepublishing.com.

Skyhorse® and Skyhorse Publishing® are registered trademarks of Skyhorse Publishing, Inc.®, a Delaware corporation.

Visit our website at www.skyhorsepublishing.com.

10 9 8 7 6 5 4 3

Library of Congress Cataloging-in-Publication Data is available on file.

Cover design by Tom Lau
Cover photo credit: iStockphoto

Print ISBN: 978-1-5107-1308-6
Ebook ISBN: 978-1-5107-1314-7

Printed in China

TABLE OF CONTENTS

PART II: GUNS AND GEAR

PART III: FEATURES

EDITOR'S NOTE

Last year, *Guns & Ammo*'s parent company, the Outdoor Sportsman Group (OSG), entered into an agreement with Skyhorse Publishing to start doing books together. Many OSG titles are involved: *Petersen's Hunting, Wildfowl, RifleShooter, Shooting Times, Handguns,* and, of course, *Guns & Ammo*. The plan is to take articles from the various magazines, then make them into one-topic books. As I write this, a copy of the first book in this new venture, *Petersen's Hunting Guide to Big Game,* was just delivered to our offices. *Petersen's Hunting Guide to Whitetail Deer* will be next.

Guns & Ammo has an exciting lineup of books on the way, too. The first, *Guns & Ammo's Guide to Sniping,* was a natural. It's a hot topic, interest is growing, and *Guns & Ammo* has a lineup of recognized experts in the field, writing about everything from new guns and loads, to amazing optics, to tactics and techniques designed to help you shoot more accurately at greater distances. They have the experts—real snipers in this case—so you need to pay attention to what they say. They know what they're talking about.

Future *Guns & Ammo* books will include the *Guns & Ammo's Guide to Concealed Carry,* the *Guns & Ammo's Guide to AK-47s,* and the *Guns & Ammo's Guide to AR-15s.* But first things first: please check out the *Guide to Sniping.* Editor-in-chief Eric Poole helped pick out the majority of stories in this book, written by such tried-and-true G&A authors as Tom Beckstrand, Jeff Hoffman, and Todd Hodnett. We'd like to know what you think of it. We're in this for the long haul, and want to help you build up a library that's loaded with books you want.

Jay Cassell
Editorial Director
Skyhorse Publishing
www.skyhorsepublishing.com

PART I
TACTICS

MYT
OF LONG RANGI

SLAYING EARLY SNIPER LORE.

BY Todd Hodnett

I grew up like most country boys, I suppose. Sitting on the floor in front of the TV anxiously anticipating the voice of Curt Gowdy on "The American Outdoorsmen." I still get chills as I remember his intro to the show. I couldn't wait for my horizon to expand to places I couldn't even imagine and watch as hunters chased game of far-away lands—or so it seemed to me, a young boy from the Texas Panhandle.

I dug into "Field and Stream" to learn as much as I could from any source I could find about my passion for hunting. I think that most of us found our base knowledge this way. Unfortunately, a lot of this information was not as correct as we might want to admit, but it was, in my opinion, the best we could do at the time. Now than it would be in ammo to gather dope the old-fashioned way.

I know that some of these thoughts will ruffle a few feathers, but like I tell my students, let the bullet tell the truth. It doesn't get to vote, and it never lies. Go out and test your doubts. As I always say, "Question everything."

at 100 meters (or even 500 meters). It seems to be a built-in excuse, as I have heard guys on the line say, "It's gotten hotter, and I did not make a correction for it, and that is why I missed." Now, this could be true at distance, but not at 400 meters. These are a few numbers to review:

Myths that we've been taught can and must be challenged. The field is a great place to put many of these tales to rest. There is no better way to determine if a principle is true than trying it for oneself.

understand, I am not knocking the gentlemen who gathered this data and developed our shooting manuals from this information, but we have to admit that as we advance in any field we find new ways that are better, and sometimes we discover that what we believed was not as correct as we had imagined.

With the advent of ballistic computers, now anyone can have the knowledge of a lifetime of rounds put downrange and all the information that 100-plus data books could ever hope to give us. It is all at our fingertips, and the cost is usually less

Let's start with some common misconceptions.

EVERY 20 DEGREES FAHRENHEIT MOVES YOUR BULLET ONE MOA

Now, this one has a lot of issues. For one, I believe people are thinking about Density Altitude (DA), but when you talk temperature and ammo, you have to think about the temperature sensitivity of the powder. But let's just stay with the DA issue. This old myth is pretty close if you are looking at the deviation you might see in a 20-degree temp change at 1,000 yards, but not

	50°	70°
900m hold	11.48	11.16
500m hold	3.97	3.82
300m hold	1.46	1.44

900m: .28 mils, or nearly one MOA difference

EVERY 1,000 FEET OF ELEVATION CHANGE, WE GET ONE MOA SHIFT

Again, this is pretty close at 1,000 yards, but I have students approach me consistently who believe that they will see a change in POI at 100 meters when we move 5,000 feet up from the region where we zeroed the rifle.

So instead of telling them there is no change, I started asking all the guys to make sure they zeroed their rifles before they show up at my High Angle class, which has a base camp at 5,000 feet. When the students arrive, I tell them to confirm zero, and some will ask how much shift they should expect. I tell them to re-zero then test their zero upon arrival back home. They report back that they don't have any shift overall.

	Sea level	1,000 ft
900m	11.16	10.86
500m	3.82	3.76
300m	1.44	1.43

900m: .3 mils, or one MOA difference

Gathering dope can provide valuable feedback, but it is a time-consuming and costly endeavor. Our time and effort is put to better use truing.

the rifle if there is a shift. To their astonishment, there is no change. My "test" has been continuous since 2005. I also tell the students to zero their rifle before they go home and

So, as you can see, at 1,000 yards or the equivalent 914 meters, the DA change shown in the last two examples result in the one MOA shift, but only at 1,000 yards.

MYTHS ABOUT GATHERING DOPE VERSUS TRUING

Guys ask me that if they have the chance, is gathering dope more accurate than truing? Gathering dope is not a bad thing, it's just not needed anymore. The dope can be as accurate as the shooter and his attention to all the variables. However, the easier and more scientific way is to "true." What I mean by this is to find the algorithm the bullet is flying on and make the ballistic computer match. The way we do this is to zero the rifle at whatever range you desire and then shoot at a target that is near transonic for optimum results. The target doesn't have to be at trans, but this will give the best result. When you shoot, you will find the actual hold for the target by seeing where your bullet is hitting and making second-shot corrections. Then with all the correct atmospheric conditions accounted for, we change the muzzle velocity to find the correct algorithm.

Now let me explain why we don't true the BC. Bullet companies have two main ways to sell their product. One is the terminal ballistic properties, or how well the bullet expands or penetrates through a certain

Truing allows us to have accurate ballisitic solutions across an infinite selection of ranges. With accurate data on atmospherics and range, truing will get us hits on target faster than any other approach.

material. The other is the external ballistic properties. This is how well the bullet flies through the air and can be aged on its stability and/or drag, due to what we use as a BC number. In 1877, Charles Krupp came up with what we refer to as a BC number. As just a quick explanation, he shot a one-pound bullet that was one inch in diameter, and due to its performance he declared it a one-BC bullet. We are still using this numeric system today. Actually, it still works very well. It just gives us an indication of how efficient our bullet is in flight. You can find the actual BC of your bullet if you shoot, say, 10 rounds through a chronograph and then note the actual impact point at transonic range, then true the BC this time instead of muzzle velocity. This is the only time we might true the BC in supersonic ranges, and this is why. I have heard that one should true the BC at 300 meters. Let me show you why one should never do this. Let's say you shoot at a target at 300 meters and the bullet strikes .15 mil higher than you planned. This is only half MOA or 1.77 inches. If you try to true the algorithm to even this slight change at 300 meters, with a .308 .475 BC, you will find that you now have a BC of over .7, and everyone knows this is ludicrous.

Even though the BC may be slightly in error, the MV will self-calibrate to give us the actual algorithm. I really don't care if the MV is correct, but I do care if all my holds are correct. I show my students that you can take an actual real algorithm with real

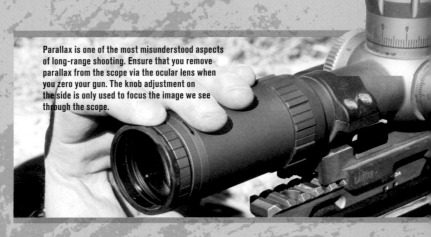

Parallax is one of the most misunderstood aspects of long-range shooting. Ensure that you remove parallax from the scope via the ocular lens when you zero your gun. The knob adjustment on the side is only used to focus the image we see through the scope.

MVs and BCs and nearly match the holds with errant MVs and errant BCs. This is what truing does for you. It's all about time of flight; it's everything. You can be pretty far off on the actual BC and then true the MV, and still you will find the actual holds for every range to be within half MOA or less. This is the beauty of what truing does for us. It will correct our algorithm for errant BCs, and we don't have to have a chrono to find the correct MV to use in the field.

MYTHS ABOUT DIALING OR HOLDS BEING MORE ACCURATE

A lot of students think that dialing is more accurate than holding. So when we start truing our rifles, they will dial. However, a good reticle is a laser-etched reticle by a CAD machine, and these are very accurate if done by a quality company. One thing for sure is that a lot of companies have problems making turrets that dial correctly. I can remember growing up doing the "Box Drill." This is where you dial a mil up then a mil right, then down and then left. This should then place your round back where you started. Most scopes can do this. However, the

test I run on my scopes today is a little different. I use a CATS target from Horus. This target has lines marked at every mil for a certain distance, either 100 meters or 100 yards. I place it on a 4x8 piece of Sheetrock, and it fully covers it. Then I confirm zero on the square at the bottom and then start the test. I will then dial 4 mils right, 10 mils up, 5 down, 10 up and now I am at 15 mils up. Then 8 left, then 10 down, 5 up, 10 down and then last, 4 right. This will place the bullet back at my starting point, and every shot is tracked for accuracy. Some scopes can track perfectly, and some have huge issues. This is one of the most important tests you can do if you ever intend to dial. I have seen scopes more than a mil off at 15 mils up, but in the first five mils of dialing up, the scope looked like it was OK.

The main point to take away from this is that dialing is never more accurate than holding, if you have a reticle that allows you to hold to a closely subtended point.

By the way, if your scope doesn't dial correctly and you true the MV to the dialed mil instead of a hold, when you hold you could have deviation in impact from the suggested hold. At this point you should run a quick test. When you are out shooting and you find an exact hold for a target and you're doing head shots with eight mils of elevation, dial your eight mils in and see if you can still do head shots with your crosshairs. If not, your scope is not dialing correctly.

BULLETS TUMBLE AT SUBSONIC

I will not say that bullets can't tumble at transonic or subsonic ranges, but I will say that if you are shooting a good bullet with the proper twist rate, your bullet will not tumble.

Every week in my class we shoot .308 calibers out to a mile. This is twice the range at which the bullet hits transonic and on average 500 meters past subsonic, and we have seen zero problems with bullets tumbling. I actually placed an 8-foot by 8-foot target up and had a student shoot a group at every 100 meters all the way out to 1,910 meters. We never had a bullet tumble into the Sheetrock target.

The reason your bullet may tumble is the lack of gyroscopic stability retention at the ranges of transonic or subsonic. A better or faster twist rate can impart the amount of spin needed to give this stability.

PARALLAX

This is one of the biggest problems I encounter with all my students. I believe that good young eyes adjust so fast that a reticle that looks blurry at first will become clear so fast that the younger eyes have a hard time with parallax. So let's go over how to set parallax and what the myth is.

The correct way to *set* parallax is with the ocular lens. This is the one nearest your eye. The parallax adjustment on the side or on the front of your scope is for the clarity of the target. It will *adjust* the overall parallax for the shot at any range desired. But if the parallax was not set properly when you zeroed the gun, it can affect the result of your shots at longer ranges. I have seen guys set the ocular to what they think is a clear reticle and then just turn the side parallax knob until they no longer see movement between the crosshair and the target. This is *not* setting the parallax correctly unless the target and the reticle are crisp. I have heard guys say that if the reticle is clear and the target is a little blurry and there is no movement of the reticle on the target as you move your head this is as good as you can get the scope, but the parallax is removed. This is not true. If so, you would have to have the same amount of blur on every subsequent target at all the different ranges.

There are many more myths out there. Don't even believe me. Be smart and test everything. Go out and put it to the test. The bullet never lies and doesn't get to vote, but the truth will set you free from all misconceptions of the past.

UNUSUAL SHOOTING POSITIONS

MORE TOOLS FOR THE TOOLBOX.
BY CAYLEN E. WOJCIK // PHOTOS BY DEREK MCDONALD/SUREFIRE

Unusual shooting positions can encompass just about anything your imagination can come up with. The birth of an unusual shooting position is usually the result of a worst-case scenario becoming reality for a sniper. Most often, these types of positions are indicative of combative shooting or hunting, and shooting in nontypical positions is difficult. It tests your ability to apply the core fundamentals of marksmanship and remain consistent through a wide range of positions and personal comfort levels. Once you begin to practice these positions and see how accurate you can be, they become a constructive challenge.

As precision rifle shooters, our training usually begins in the supported prone position or on the bench utilizing some type of gizmo that allows us to maximize accuracy from our rifles and ammunition. Obviously, we can purchase the finest components in a rifle, its optic and ammunition. However, in order for this package to reach its full potential, we need to properly manipulate the trigger. For some shooters, the bench is satisfying. For military and law enforcement snipers, seldom comes an opportunity to make a shot happen in perfect-world prone. I believe that most shooters get themselves into a certain comfort zone, and it's within this comfort zone that the shooter feels content with his performance. For an operational sniper, once the rifle is zeroed and the fundamentals are learned, it's time to test one's ability as a marksman—and that means getting out of prone.

POSITION EFFECTS

Before going into a few of the unusual positions, we first need to discuss the mechanics of our optic. Without a doubt, being proficient with a scoped rifle system means understanding eye relief, line of sight (or optical axis) and parallax. Proper sight alignment results from the shooter

seeing a full field of view of the reticle, which means that the shooter's eye is the proper distance from the objective lens and perfectly centered along the scope's optical axis. Generally speaking, when a shooter sets up his rifle for getting into the prone, he gets settled and moves the scope in the rings to obtain proper eye relief. He also raises or lowers the rifle's cheekpiece to obtain that perfect alignment. Now, this works fine for the prone position, but what happens to the stockweld as he moves into different shooting positions? It changes.

Some positions change a shooter's cheekweld with the stock more than others, while some don't seem to affect it

at all. The point is to be aware of the potential for change and take notice. The cheekpiece height may be perfect in the prone, but how's it looking in a low kneeling or a sitting position? No matter the scenario, you must always strive to achieve the lowest position possible. Operationally, several things—such as time, available cover and the distance of the engagement—will dictate the type of position we can achieve. The closer we are to the ground, the more we can use its inherent stability. When you do get into position, be sure to use your bone structure for support. Bones don't get tired like muscles do.

HAWKINS

In the realm of unusual shooting positions, pretty much anything goes. There are a couple of positions, however, that visually stand out as being unusual but are actually quite normal for some shooters. One is the Hawkins position. The Hawkins is one of the oldest prone supported positions I know of. How far back it goes is unknown to me. Some would say that its name is derived from the Hawkins muzzleloader fond of trappers and bear hunters used throughout the mid-nineteenth century. Regardless, it is a position that is still taught to modern snipers of the British army. Interestingly, it is a required position as part of their known-distance course of fire for qualification.

One of the advantages of the Hawkins that immediately stands out is that the shooter can get extremely low to the ground. As a matter of fact, the rifle stock is actually making contact with the ground. This makes for a very low profile, ideal for snipers attempting to remain concealed. The shooter would move into a position, and once satisfied with it, dig a small trench into which he would place the stock's toe. This becomes the rear support. The front support is nothing more than the shooter's fist of the nonfiring hand. Most of these snipers are taught to grasp the rifle's sling at the front swivel. Elevation adjustments (if needed) are usually small. A simple squeeze of the fist will result in an elevated point of aim, and vice versa for

a drop in elevation. The shooter's armpit is actually over the top of the heel of the stock. Eye relief and sight picture are an important consideration in this position. When the rifle is fired, recoil control is taken care of by the earth, so follow-up shots can be made quickly.

The limitations of this position as it relates to other prone positions are few, but still present. The ability to make large elevation adjustments is virtually nonexistent. Anything lower than a flattened hand and you've got the rifle on the ground. Obviously, shooting uphill just isn't going to happen here. By digging a trench for the stock, the shooter is limited by the amount of traverse, and, of course, eye relief and sight alignment present potential problems. The Hawkins is very accurate nonetheless.

MODIFIED BUFFALO HUNTER

On one end of the position spectrum, two positions are probably the most unusual you have ever seen. The first is what I like to call the Modified Buffalo Hunter. Ever see an artist's rendition of a buffalo hunt in the 1870s? If you have, you've probably seen a shooter lying on his back with the long barrel of his Sharps resting in the crook of his crossed legs and the stock seemingly buried in his armpit. This was also a popular position with long-range competitors of that same era. With a scoped rifle, there are some important considerations, particularly the ridiculously long eye relief.

Ideally, this position is best utilized with a pack on,

looking downhill and when you don't have the time to get into a prone position. The rifle's stock is in contact with the shoulder, and the shooting hand grips the rifle as normal. The nonshooting hand grasps the rifle's sling, and the shooter should pull the rifle into his shoulder, further adding support. The knees should be bent and ankles crossed, allowing the rifle stock or barrel to rest in this crook. Bringing your crossed ankles closer to your body or pushing them farther out can help to make minor elevation adjustments.

SIDE SADDLE

Another position, which I've dubbed the Side Saddle, is also useful in very hasty downhill shooting situations. As with the Modified Buffalo Hunter, it's very helpful to have a pack on your back to give you something to lean against. The shooter lies on his side and assumes something resembling the fetal position. The legs are bent at the knees, and the rifle rests on the upper thigh. The use of a sling really makes this position stable.

Detach the sling from its rear anchor, and tightly wrap it around your upper thigh twice. Grasp the rifle as normal with your shooting hand, and let your elbow rest naturally. Use your nonshooting hand to grasp the rear of the stock,

and manipulate the rifle so that you can obtain some semblance of sight alignment and sight picture. Eye relief is nonexistent here, and the shooter should dial back the magnification on the optic to make the exit pupil as large as possible. In order to make an accurate shot, every effort must be made to keep the exit pupil centered within the ocular lens of the scope. With practice, you'll be surprised at how far out you can be accurate. The shooter should also consider the effects of recoil in this position since the only thing that keeps the rifle from moving is the sling wrapped around your leg.

BUDDY SUPPORT

Other positions that can be considered unusual, though effective, are buddy-supported positions. Not employed very often, they are useful in situations that don't allow the shooter to obtain a better support. Buddy-support positions can be assumed anywhere from the standing to the prone. The key to maximizing the support in these positions is the use of a sling and teamwork. Traditionally, the observer

drives the shooter. However, buddy-supported positions require the shooter to drive the observer. Buddy breathing is necessary to control, meaning that the shooter must tell the observer when to breathe in, breathe out and hold to make the shot. The observer can also assist in the support by grasping the sling of the rifle system and applying downward tension. When using a buddy-support position in the prone, use the back of your thighs as the rifle's rest. Although on his back appears to be the most stable way for

PRONE

SITTIN

STANDING

Photos by Derek McDonald/Surefire

your observer to lie, his breathing cycle creates excessive movement for the shooter.

SLINGS

One item that I always have on my rifle is a sling. There are literally hundreds of sling designs out there, and you must pick the one that suits you and fits your needs. I prefer to use a Tactical Intervention Quick-Cuff. It offers great features at a reasonable price, and it's highly functional. Traditional sling-supported positions are obviously not unusual, but I don't think an article on shooting positions would be complete without touching on them. A sling is a valuable tool that's all too often forgotten in the realm of precision rifle shooting.

With the advent of bipods, there wasn't really a need to learn the traditional loop sling. Granted, bipods allow us to mitigate the felt effects of recoil by permitting the shooter to place his body directly in line with the bore, therefore allowing the weight of the body to distribute the energy evenly. Bipods are mechanical, and according to Mr. Murphy's law, they are therefore bound to fail at some point. If you have a sling on your rifle and are trained in the sling-supported positions, you will remain an effective force multiplier in the event that you don't have the luxury of a bipod in the field.

JUST FOR YOU

When using a sling-supported position, know and understand that everyone's body mechanics are different. What works for one shooter may not work well for you. I know from personal experience that the low kneeling position offers more support than the high kneeling, as the body's center of gravity is closer to the ground. No matter how much stretching I do, I can't get into a low kneeling position. My ankle just doesn't roll that way. On the range, I used to envy those on the 300-yard line who could get into that rock-solid low kneeling.

I encourage everyone to break away from your comfort zone and push the limits to see where your limits really lie. I think you'll be surprised as to how accurate you can be once you settle in. For military and law enforcement snipers, not stepping outside that comfort zone could cost you your life or someone else's life that you're charged with protecting. Anything can get you killed in combat, including doing nothing. When the day comes to utilize a tool from your box and an unusual situation presents itself, pulling together an unusual shooting position won't seem so unfamiliar if you practice.

KNEELING

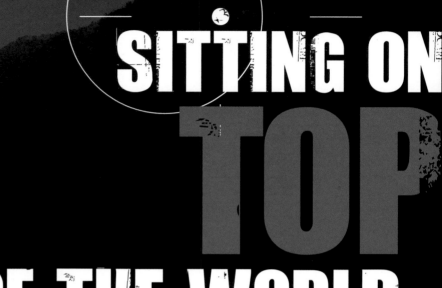

SITTING ON TOP OF THE WORLD

UNCONVENTIONAL HIGH-ANGLE SHOOTING POSITIONS.

BY SGM KYLE LAMB (RET.)

When we use the term "conventional shooting positions," what we should really say is "shooting positions for range and competition use only." While conducting training with predominantly high-level military and law enforcement personnel, I rarely have a student who has engaged the enemy from the prone shooting position. This speaks volumes about how we should actually conduct our training. I am not saying you should never use the prone position, but you should have a more realistic outlook on how you might possibly engage a threat.

This is especially true when operating in a mountainous environment. Most extreme terrain will not allow you to get into a normal range-shooting position without feeling like you're going to roll down a hill. Or you may feel as though your range of movement is severely limited. This is important if you are engaging targets that are not static, and most real threats are not static. I am sure there are many Marines and soldiers who can attest to this.

There are several features your high-angle shooting position should allow. **ABILITY TO ENGAGE MULTIPLE THREATS QUICKLY.** It is important that your position allows you to engage several threats if necessary or at least be able to scan a large sector of fire. If several shooters are in position with large fields of fire that overlap, you will be more effective as an assault or sniper element. **STABILITY.** Shooting under adverse conditions does not change the fact that you need to be stable to shoot effectively. The selected position should be relatively stable, and depending on the range, you may need to cheat even more to get as stable as possible. **SUSTAINABILITY.** You don't know how long you will need to be in this position. Sustainability is a huge issue from the prone position from high angles. If you have to crane your neck or arch your back to get into the prone position, the

position will become unsustainable pretty quickly. **COMFORT.** Comfort is also key. A little discomfort from a tight sling or a rock poking you in the back isn't what I mean. I'm talking about cramps that will hit you when you least expect them and prevent you from making the shot you need. **MOBILITY.** Static positions are important, but you may need to move quickly in and out of this position—quickly into position if you have a target of

Rifle is clamped to inside of the knee, sling is tight to enhance the shooting position. Ejection port is clear.

opportunity to neutralize, and quickly out of position to get better cover if the enemy is engaging your position. **ABILITY TO SEE THE THREAT.** If you can't see what you are shooting at, you'll never hit it. Makes sense, but I often have shooters get into a downhill prone position who then can't get a shot off because they have lost sight of the target. They then must rotate into a new position to try to get a shot off. This may work on steel targets, but if you are hunting people you might not get that opportunity again.

Kneeling Position or Brace Kneeling

When using the ground, rocks or trees for support in the kneeling position, it is important to switch knees in order to get better support for your rifle. It is also important to keep your profile as low as possible. To help attain this you should try to drop your elbow in front of your knee. If you have to keep your elbow on your knee, that's OK, but you will not be as stable and may present a better target to the threat.

This position works well regardless of the angle of the shot. Up or down, you would be able to find a suitable position.

There may come a time when you have to shoot from a position that more closely resembles your conventional kneeling, with the support-side knee up to support the front of your rifle. This position is OK, but being able to get support for the front and the rear of the rifle is more desirable.

High-Angle Sitting Positions

Standard sitting positions can get very sketchy in no time if you are in a precarious position. I always feel like I'm going to roll down the hill if I cross my legs as I would for a standard sitting position. While wearing normal field gear, you may not be able to get into these positions. Once you're in position, is it sustainable and comfortable?

I feel more stable and comfortable if I let my support-side knee be used as a brace and the magazine of the rifle is braced to my leg. One of the most important elements to this high-angle sitting position is the sling. You should have your sling tightened down to aid with stability. It's like having another set of hands helping hold the rifle in place. The strong-side knee is laid to the side to give

The elbow is dropped in front of the knee for additional stability. This will also help to enhance sustainability.

Stacking your feet looks crazy but works extremely well in severe terrain. Bipod is used to clamp rifle to the shooter's toe.

Ensure that the barrel will clear cover. The elbow rests on the knee for a rock-solid position.

you a more relaxed position. This will also help keep you in place if the terrain is severely steep.

Last, it is important to keep the shooting elbow down in order to keep a smaller profile if shooting around cover or concealment. Bad guys track on movement, so leave the elbow down and don't move it around when trying to stay out of sight. If you require better recoil control, try to grip the rifle a little tighter with the support hand that is around the front of your knee. It should help.

Once you are in your sitting position, if you feel stable and comfortable with your shooting-side knee up, place your elbow on that knee or thigh for more

support and stability.

Stacking Your Feet

One of my favorites—and a true crowd-pleaser in the Carbine and Sniper Courses at Viking Tactics–is the stacked-feet position. This position looks crazy when you first see it, but after getting into the position, almost all of the shooters we meet like it. You may think you have to be a Las Vegas stripper to get into this position. I haven't touched my toes without bending my knees since I was seven, yet I can wrap myself into this position, so you just might want to give it a try as well. You should be aware that this position works much better if you are at a high angle than if you're on a flat surface.

If you are using a bipod or a vertical grip on your gun, this would be a good time to use it more as a handle than as a support. As you can see in the photo, the shooter has grabbed the bottom of his boot, and then wrapped his thumb around the bipod to hold everything in place during the firing process. You don't need a bipod or vertical grip for this position, but it definitely

helps. If you prefer to choke up on your rifle by grabbing the front of your magazine well, that will not work at all for this position. It is also important that you don't let the barrel touch your toes, because this will destroy your accuracy. Once again, ensure that you have tightened your sling to help hold all the pieces and parts together to enhance your accuracy.

If you are in a high-angle situation, first and foremost on your mind should be finding great cover. If you can position yourself above a rock, you will be prepared for the worst-case scenario. You should also note that simply using one foot for support might be the key.

Get a Good Rangefinder

If you find yourself in one of these positions, it's time to get a true horizontal range from you to the target with your rangefinder. I prefer to use a Leupold RX-1000 simply because it tells me what the distance is that my bullet will be affected by gravity. I prefer this technique to trying to bust out the calculator to figure out angle and cosine to compute a distance. But that's another article.

So the next time you find yourself "sitting on top of the world," grab a handful of rifle, lean into it and squeeze the trigger.

PR

ECISION
RIFLE SERIES

WHEN YOU'RE SERIOUS ABOUT SHOOTING A RIFLE, THIS IS YOUR FINISHING SCHOOL.

BY TOM BECKSTRAND

PHOTOS BY BARRY EVANS AND ROSS MARTIN

Being a gun hack comes with a unique set of first-world problems. Namely, I'm always shooting other peoples' guns. Last summer, I got a phone call asking me to compete in a Precision Rifle Series (PRS) match so my publisher could film a TV episode around it. It sounded like fun, so I rogered up and made my way out west. My rifle? A bone-stock Tikka T3 Tactical chambered in .223 Remington I zeroed the day before the match (.223-caliber rifles were their own class for this particular match).

The two days I spent competing out in New Mexico were a ton of fun. Competitors fired 27 stages under some very dusty and windy conditions. It was a great way to see how your equipment held up while both you and Mother Nature beat on it. Some rifles locked up, a few scopes died, and competitors created many new friendships. I met a bunch of really good dudes and was beaten decisively by some amazing shooters. I was hooked.

HOW IT WORKS

The idea for the PRS came about fairly recently. In 2011, Rich Emmons and Kevin Elpers had the idea of creating a national circuit where rifle shooters from around the country could compete against one another and be ranked according to their performance. Rich said, "I wanted to create a competition series that allowed guys to compete in fair and reputable events on a mini-circuit."

In pursuit of this goal, Rich and Kevin coordinated their efforts with members of the shooting industry and teamed up with select match directors from around the country. Match directors who were running quality long-range matches were approached and solicited for their input on how to create the circuit and standardize the matches. A few directors teamed with Rich and Kevin to form a board of directors, and they created the scoring system the PRS uses.

The first full PRS season ran in 2012 with a total membership of 164 shooters. There were 12 PRS-sanctioned matches that year, and more than $20,000 was paid out in prize money at the Finale. The series also gave out approxi- mately $100,000 in prizes off the Finale prize table. The match is open to the top 50 ranked shooters on the circuit, and the location has changed each year so far. The first Finale was held at Rifles Only in Texas.

In 2013, there were 14 sanc- tioned matches and 171 members. The year 2013 also saw the intro- duction of the Semi-Pro class to give newcomers to the sport an op- portunity to compete against those with a similar level of experience. There were only two divisions in the PRS last year, Pro and Semi-Pro.

This year has seen a number of changes, and all of them make a great program even better. The Semi-Pro category has been replaced with the Long-Range Hunter category, designed for newcomers to the sport and hunters who don't want to compete all the time but recognize the training value of a good shooting match. Members of the Long- Range Hunter division only have to shoot two sanctioned matches to get ranked and be eligible for the Finale.

The PRS is working with local clubs to allow club teams to compete against each other as well. The Club Championship was held in February, with seven clubs comprising 42 shooters coming from around the country to shoot the match in Oklahoma. This is also a good way for new shooters to ease their way into national competition.

THE BEST WAY TO GET TO KNOW YOUR RIFLE IS **TO GET OUT AND COMPETE WITH IT.**

Photo by Barry Evans and Ross Martin

WHAT'S IT LIKE?

My first PRS match was for a TV show, and I was woefully unprepared. That particular match had a .223 division, and I chose to compete in it. My rationale was that, since I was competing with a factory rifle and could only choose between .223 and .308, it would be better to compete in a class where everyone's ballistic coefficients (BCs) sucked a lot (like the .223 does) versus shooting in the Open class with a .308 and being the only guy with a gun whose BC sucked just a little. (The 6mm and 6.5mm cartridges dominate the Open class, or Pro Series, because the BCs are high and the recoil is low.)

The learning curve for my first match was steep, and a lot of things went wrong. I knew it wasn't a great idea to compete with a rifle I'd never fired before while using a scope and reticle that were also new to me. Regardless of what rifle and scope you have or use, being familiar with your equipment and knowing how to make it perform ultimately determine how well we shoot. That statement is true whether or not we compete.

Knowing our rifle and shooting it well will get us into the top half of any PRS match. No amount of money spent on super-trick guns and gear will compensate for a lack of effort and training. Allow me to steal a quote from the Four Special Operations Forces Truths: "Humans are more important than hardware." Know thy rifle, and shoot it well.

PRS matches challenge all types of shooters by presenting targets in real-world scenarios.

Photos by Barry Evans and Ross Martin

Whimpering and hand-wringing over caliber, reticle and ancillary gear only wastes money and effort. Once we shoot a few matches, we'll have that stuff all figured out.

The best way to get to know your rifle is to get out and compete with it. The PRS matches are a ton of fun and allow us to shoot courses of fire with which we are totally unfamiliar. That's the best way to learn. Shooting from the prone over and over again will only make us good at shooting prone. The same goes if we only shoot off a bench.

PRS matches have us shooting off and over barricades, from gabled roofs, offhand, through car windows, off swaying platforms that mimic a boat, out of simulated sewer pipes, around walls and occasionally from the prone. It is a graduate-level education in positional shooting that we can get no other way. It will absolutely make each one of us a better shooter.

We'll learn because we'll make mistakes and find out what doesn't

Don't forget your handgun. Precision Rifle Series matches include stages designed for your sidearm as well as your rifle.

Photos by Barry Evans and Ross Martin

Above, left to right: Dustin Morris took third place, Bryan Morgan took first, and Ryan Castle took second in Woody's North Carolina Match. Right: Mark Gordon, owner of Short Action Customs, placed 11th.

work. We'll learn because we're rubbing elbows with the best shooters in the nation, and they make it look easy. Watch them, and learn from them. I'm all for attending courses and getting formal instruction, but only from guys who shoot well. An instructor who won't shoot in front of his students is a poor instructor. At the PRS matches, we get a parade of exceptional shooters who we get to watch in action. Once they're done shooting, ask them how they did what they did, and they'll tell you.

The matches I've fired permitted me to get to know a few of the top-ranked guys on the circuit, and I've learned a bunch from them already. I was lucky enough to get squadded with Dustin Morris; his dad, Todd;

Smiles are big and frequent at these events.

and Wade Stuteville for my first match. They were very polite and helpful, and none of them knew me from Adam. Dustin and I laugh

about it now, but he says it took them half a day to figure out that I was hosting the show that brought the cameras out. They befriended me and knew nothing about me. It'll be like that for each one of you.

Of course, match regulars know one another and will want to socialize with their friends. A little social skill makes it easier to approach strangers and strike up a conversation, so we should all try to put our best foot forward and make an effort to integrate. The important thing to remember is that if you love rifles and shooting them, these are your people. They love guns and shooting as much as you do. Personalities vary, but I've met a lot of guys at the matches, and only one was a wannabe sniper who I didn't like. (Some guys you just dislike the first time you see them. It's rare, but it happens. I'll get over it.)

TALKING TO THE CHAMP

I called Dustin Morris to ask him a few questions about the PRS as part of my preparation for this article. I got to know Dustin and his dad, Todd, at that first match and admired both men immediately. I was fortunate enough to spend a couple of days shooting alongside them. They are polite, friendly and Lord, have mercy, can they make a rifle sing! Dustin finished the 2013 season as the number-one-ranked shooter on the PRS. He knows what he's doing. Todd wasn't far behind him.

Dustin and Todd are farmers from Louisiana. They were never black-ops ninjas; but they grew up around guns and really like to shoot them. So often people think you have to be a former Special Ops guy or a Marine sniper to be competitive. Nothing could be further from the truth. The best shooters in any discipline are regular guys who shoot because they love it. Not every cop or soldier really loves to shoot. They have a lot of other tasks they also have to be good at, and shooting is only one of them. It's why you don't see a lot of those types at these kinds of matches. Also, nothing is more humbling to a barrel-chested, steely eyed freedom fighter than to go to a match and get beaten soundly by an overweight, middle-aged plumber. It stings a little. Ask me how I know.

Dustin was full of good advice for new shooters thinking about taking on the PRS. He started competing just six years ago when he went to his first precision rifle match in southern Alabama. In his words, "I went to the school of hard knocks." He started with a left-handed Remington 700 chambered in 6XC with a Nightforce scope that had a reticle designed for benchrest shooting but was horrible for a precision rifle match.

The most intimidating point for Dustin was when he pulled up to his first match and everyone was dressed like GI Joe. (It is a good idea to wear clothes that hide dirt stains well, are loose and allow for freedom of movement. Often, these clothes look like military cast-offs.) He stepped out of the truck in blue jeans and a collared polo. The next time you see Dustin at a match with sponsor logos all over his shooting shirt, remember that he was once a newbie, too.

When I asked Dustin what was the most important lesson he learned over the past six years, he answered, "Shooting is 80 to 90 percent mental. It's really important to know your dope backward and forward. Sooner or later, you'll have to shoot on instinct, and you either know your hold or you don't."

He recommends that new shooters just show up and shoot. "Try to be as prepared as possible, so know your rifle's dope. If you do that, you totally eliminate all vertical error and just have to worry about the wind." It's the "school of hard knocks" approach, but no other method will allow you to learn more and learn faster.

My goal is to hit three PRS matches a year and, hopefully, one day soon qualify for the Finale. Like many of you, there are a lot of things that compete for my time. Family, faith and job responsibilities all require our attention. Making sure things are right at home should be our highest priority. However, once those obligations are met, I'm happiest with a rifle in my hand, just like many of you. So, Lord willing and the creek don't rise, I'll see you at a match sometime soon.

WHO'S YOUR SPOTTER?

BY JEFF HOFFMAN

PHOTO BY MARK FINGAR

It's common knowledge in the sniping community that the spotter is the most experienced member of the team. He makes the observations and calculations and directs the shot. The title of this article might be provocative to some, comforting to others. The Indian Chief Tecumseh wisely wrote, "Trouble no man about his religion." My intent is not to convert anyone but to provide thoughts that might help snipers navigate ROE (rules of engagement) beyond those provided by your command. The thoughts expressed here are mine. If you see something of value here, good. If you don't, I'm the one to give hell to, not the publisher.

I often pray on call-outs. I do not wear religion on my sleeve, as I have often seen that those who make a great show of religion use it for their own purposes. I think it's important to be in communication with God, just as it's important to be in good communication with the rest of your team. ROE for the team depends on the law and the subject's actions. ROE for God's Law depends also on what's in your heart.

If there are those here who don't believe in God, that's your choice, but understand, you must have something solid to rely on to make righteous decisions of life and death. Your personal desire and emotion are insufficient as standards for the task of deciding whether to take a human life. You need to find that "rock," whatever it is, in addition to your organization's ROE prior to looking at another human through your scope. In this article, I will relate three call-outs where I asked for an ROE check from my "Spotter."

BACK AGAIN

This was not the first time we had been here. The prior barricade situation had been resolved without injuries, but we all knew we would be back. This time the suspect was actively firing from the house. I took a chance and took up the same position as I had some months before, 40 yards directly in front of side one, looking right in the front door. It was propped open, for the suspect's benefit, not ours.

He didn't intend to give us an unobstructed shot. Rather, he was planning to eventually stand in the front door, level his shotgun and shoot whomever he could see. He had been shooting all night without hitting anyone. I could hear the shotgun pellets whistle through the trees above me. I had good concealment but, as is often the case, zilch for cover. I used a few pieces of wood from behind the shed for approach, but otherwise I had only darkness to protect me. The wood was more concealment than cover, but you take what you can get.

There was no hostage, so we just had a barricade situation with a nut shooting up the neighborhood. His fire was ineffective so far, but sooner or later he was likely to hit someone. After a few hours, the subject told negotiators he could see a cop and planned to kill him. That was the last straw, and Command gave the order for snipers to engage at the first opportunity. I looked at the front door again and calculated the odds of me being the one to take the shot when the subject came to the open front door to shoot. He was getting bolder. I felt there was about an 80 percent probability that the doorway—my doorway—was where the shot would be offered.

I then thought to myself, *What is the chance I will shoot him when he presents himself in the doorway?* and immediately knew the answer—100 percent. Then I said a prayer: *God, if this guy has a guardian angel, put him on the job, because this guy is about to die.*

A short time later, the subject crossed the door, too fast to engage. I wanted a solid shot. He had no hostage, so I didn't feel the need to take the running shot. I could afford to wait for the shot I wanted. I called it out. Everyone needed to know where the subject was. I could see all the way through the house to the back sliding door. A few moments later, he reappeared, moving quickly back the other direction. I watched through the scope as the back sliding door turned opaque as it shattered from a rifle shot from the sniper team on the three side (rear) of the house.

The suspect went down like his shoes were tied together.

A RETHINK

I was TL (team leader) of a two-man sniper team posted where a body had been dumped. We were waiting for the suspect to return to the scene. He had murdered a young girl who was going door-to-door selling magazine subscriptions. He had been in the process of dumping her body down a cistern at the rural location when he was interrupted and fled. We were posted in the field in case he came back to finish the job.

It was cold lying in the frosty field 75 yards away, and I tried to keep focused. I was very angry about the crime. It hit home in a very personal way because the victim was my daughter's age. I thought of what the victim must have gone through as she died.

We had officers hidden along likely approach routes advising us of what was moving. The report came in that a blacked-out car was on its way in. I gave final directions to my teammate: "When he arrives, move into a flanking position. I will remain here, and as he reaches the point where he dumped the body, I'll challenge him and illuminate him. He'll swing toward the light with a weapon, and I'll center-punch him. You engage from your position."

I then caught myself saying a prayer: "God, let me kill this guy!" I immediately realized this was not a proper prayer. I wanted to kill the subject for revenge, not necessarily as part of my job—in my judgment, he was scum who did not deserve to live. Realizing my mistake, I regrouped and simply asked God for the capability to do my job.

Killing for my purposes would be wrong, no matter how justified the shooting would be by criminal law. God's Law also examines what is in your heart. He listens when you ask for guidance and often responds if you are listening. He can also sometimes act. This leads to the next example, which occurred last summer on another call-out.

A SKATEBOARD FROM HEAVEN?

The call-out was a hostage situation resulting from an interrupted residential burglary. The suspect was holed up in a residence with a two-year-old boy as a hostage. The subject was reported to be armed with a handgun. We deployed as best we could, with one team at the rear. Our two street-side teams were across the street from the suspect's location, one directly out the front and another, my two-man team, at an angle to the front, 93 yards from the front door. Sides were a no-go due to the proximity of other houses. As negotiations dragged on for the next five hours, solid information was still lacking. Snipers always want clear intel; it makes a difference when you are mentally preparing for a possible shot.

Questions were: Did the suspect have any reason to be there? Was this the home of a friend or relative? Was this a home invasion? Did the suspect have any relation to the hostage? Negotiators reported that the suspect claimed to be the boy's father. We could

not get confirmation of this, as the suspect was unlikely to come out for a paternity test.

Would the suspect be less likely to harm the hostage if he were the child's father? Was he actually armed? Ultimately, none of this mattered, except to help us mentally get comfortable with shooting him. After all, does a grown man need a firearm to kill a two-year-old child? No. If he was threatening to harm the hostage, did his relationship to the hostage actually matter? No. Did it matter whether the house belonged to a friend? Not at all. All that mattered was that he had the means and opportunity to harm a hostage, and that hostage was in jeopardy.

Negotiations were going nowhere. The suspect finally agreed to come out but only while carrying the child. This was unacceptable. We could not take the chance that he'd use the child as a shield while attempting to break through the perimeter and escape. We were stalled at that point, and the suspect was not presenting himself for a shot. Command made a decision.

"Negotiators, tell the suspect to come out with the child if that is the only way he will come out. Snipers, if he comes out with the child, shoot him."

I told my teammate, "Make your peace with God. We are about to kill this guy." I could hear him tactically breathing. I was doing the same. Command called. "Hoffman, are you tracking with what is happening here?"

"Yes," I replied. "The suspect is about to walk out with the child, and I am going to kill him."

"I think you got it," said Command. We got into "the bubble," where nothing existed outside of our rifles and us. The doorway negotiators were now telling the suspect to walk through. I repeated the prayer: *"God, if this guy has a guardian angel, put him on the job, because this man is about to die."* Then I added, *"I am ready to kill this man, if that is how it needs to be. But if there is another way to do this, I am open to that as well."*

About that time, I heard a clacking, rolling noise off my left shoulder. I glanced up and saw a skateboarder rolling down the road at a fast clip. As he crossed my line of fire, about six entry guys with ARs piled him up in the middle of the roadway. If there was a string line between my muzzle and the front door of the house, they were standing on it.

I called out on the radio to explain what happened and advised, "I got nothing." Command advised the negotiator to have the suspect hold up for a moment. Here's where it gets weirder. While we were sorting out the situation with the skateboarder, the suspect fell asleep. Command decided to do an entry. The team flash-banged the house and entered, apprehending the suspect and rescuing the hostage child with no injuries to anyone.

As it turns out, the suspect was not related to the child, he had no valid reason to be there, and his only weapon was a Taser, found in the house. However, his car, parked out front, was full of guns. His apparent intent was to get to his firearms and escape or go down in a blaze of glory. The child would have been in grave danger during that attempt.

The skateboarder was drunk and broke through the police line on a dare. My opinion? God sent a drunk skateboarder to save our suspect, to give him another chance to live, as he was mere seconds away from getting at least one .308 round through his cranial vault. My "Spotter" has a great sense of humor sometimes.

BEING JUDGED

I've spoken with a number of moral military snipers who, having killed many men, voice concern over how God will judge them. I have no special insights granted from above, but as anyone who knows me well will tell you, I have opinions on nearly everything. The key is that most Bibles are not well translated in this regard. The correct translation of the Sixth Commandment's "Thou shalt not kill" is "Thou shalt not murder."

The Bible is clear that it is necessary to protect the innocent, and there are times when it is necessary to kill. In the Bible, David was a very accomplished warrior and general, beginning with his slaying of Goliath. David killed thousands, yet he is described by the Lord as "a man after my own heart, who will do my will."

David was not perfect, and he was a warrior who killed many, but there is little doubt as to his place in heaven.

RUNNING A SNIPER TEAM

IF IT FEELS LIKE HERDING CATS, YOU'RE DOING IT WRONG.

BY JEFF HOFFMAN   PHOTOS BY MARK FINGAR

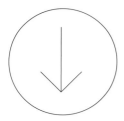

Leading a sniper team is one of the most rewarding things I've done. The responsibility, the trust of your teammates and Command, and the challenge of trying to keep up with guys 20 years younger than me are all things I will never forget. This job demands passion and a commitment to continuous work on your gear, shooting, planning and training. It also involves hanging with the most trustworthy guys in the world — fellow snipers. Here are some tricks of the trade I've learned over the years to keep things running as smoothly and safely as possible.

EDUCATE COMMAND

Make sure Command knows what to expect from your team and what it can do for them and the rest of your SRT or group. Don't assume anything. Most administrators have never been snipers. They have very little idea of what you do, how to use your assets or what you can do for them. My experience is from an LE perspective, but I think there's a good bit of common ground with military snipers.

Most administrators think a sniper is called when someone needs to be shot. They don't realize the intelligence capability a properly trained sniper team brings to the table. Ninety percent of the sniper's job is intelligence gathering. A well-trained team observes and reports invisibly. Its members are the eyes of the commander.

What is happening on-scene? Where is the suspect(s)? How many are there? What are they doing? How are they armed? How are they dressed? Are there any hostages or noncombatants? What's

the disposition/level of alertness? What's the safest approach? What are the critical terrain features providing advantage or disadvantage? Any and all information is advantageous to your commander and unit. Let your commander know what you can provide as an intel source.

Your team can provide overwatch and protect the rest of the unit. You are concealed, stationary, and in a solid platform, and with your optics and precision rifles, you can provide a high level of protection and advance warning against any threats. Snipers provide precision fire as needed, often solving problems with far less risk than when assaulters/entry personnel are used.

SELECT THE TEAM

A guy can be a great troop but still not have what it takes to be a sniper. A sniper has to be passionate about what he does. He has to want to be there. In selection, we will always take the guy who is passionate but not yet well trained over the guy who is capable but lacks enthusiasm.

There's a story I use to illustrate this. A young sailor is trying out for the Navy SEALs. The selection task involves diving into a pool and moving a concrete block to the other end of the pool. One by one, the candidates perform the task, moving the block partway, coming up for air and then going back down to move it farther. One young sailor jumps in, grabs the block and walks it down to the other end, coming up nearly drowned.

The Navy chief grabs him by the collar and screams, "What in the hell do you think you're doing? Are you trying to destroy government property by dying on me, you dumbass?" The young sailor replies, "Chief, I had to do it that way. I can't swim." The Chief responds, "With dedication like that, I don't care. We can teach you to swim!"

That's our attitude. If a guy is the right material, we can teach him to shoot.

IT'S NOT HUNTING

The snipers on some teams are assigned by Command for various reasons, including, "Bob is a hunter and knows about guns." If that is happening on your team, make it stop. Select the right people through a process, including tough physical standards, interviews, review of past records and experiences, and — maybe most important — a review by the existing snipers. Snipers have to work very closely. It's important that the new guy fits the team and is respected.

One thing we use as an absolute disqualifier is a questionable past work record. Look at sick-time use. A record of abusing sick time is a giant red flag. That is the single best indicator of dedication on a man's record.

Check his attitude, too. If he's a whiner, you don't want him. If he's frequently complaining about management, you don't want him. Same thing if he's a bragger. You want the guy who takes inward pride in getting the job done.

Nobody works as an individual on a sniper team. Some of your most important work won't be behind a rifle.

Photo by Mark Fingar

ANATOMY OF A SNIPER
Important Physical and Psychological Attributes

- Patient
- Meticulous
- Mature
- Demanding of himself
- Confident
- Dedicated
- Not a whiner
- Decisive
- Empathetic
- Moral/religious
- Intelligent
- Observant
- Articulate
- Responsible/reliable
- Proud but not a braggart
- Tough
- Independent
- Passionate about the job
- Unassuming (comes and goes without having to be noticed or making a scene)

- Methodical
- Courageous (accepts calculated risks, including criticism and review)
- Sense of humor (but not a comedian or attention-seeker)
- Imaginative (as evidenced by daydreaming or planning mentally)
- Can follow orders (but is capable of declining unsound, illegal or unreasonable, dangerous orders)
- Habitually physically fit, nonsmoker
- Experienced, including but not limited to police/military experience (life experience counts)
- Willing and comfortable with killing when necessary, even if not in personal self-defense
- Capable of boldness
- Not prone to exaggeration (the team depends on the sniper for accurate intelligence)

TRAIN THE SNIPER TEAM

To train the team, you must be able to lead them. To lead properly, there are things you need to understand. A good team, with experienced people and good leadership, can get things done very smoothly, quickly, and informally. Everyone understands his job and does it with minimal direction from the team leader. It takes time and practice to become a well-oiled machine.

In the beginning, you won't have that. Until you've established yourself as a good leader and polished your team, one of the easiest mistakes to make is to give a vague command. "Hey, guys, when you get a moment, I need you to (insert task here)."

The task will never get done. You gave direction in a casual way, which never actually got their attention. They might actually say after you walk away, "What did he say?"

Additionally, you spoke to the group as a whole — no one person had individual responsibility. Everyone thinks the other one will handle the task. You also didn't set a deadline. Technically, they did not blow you off; they just never got around to it. With you as a new leader, you need to make sure you have their attention and give direction clearly and with a deadline for performance.

They need to understand that there is a consequence for nonperformance. The penalty might be nothing more than verbally calling them on their failure to perform, but there has to be discipline. That doesn't mean you need to be a jerk about it. It just means you have to lead the team. Once you have trained them and established yourself as a respected leader, things will happen more informally. The job still gets done, and it's done smoothly and efficiently. It just takes a good team — properly trained — to make it happen.

SETTING THE EXAMPLE

In training, set the example. Aspire to be the best. Let the team know what is expected of them. Set standards. Challenge them. Represent them well to Command.

That includes getting them needed gear. You will not always get everything you want or need from the department. Get it in other ways. Snipers are pretty good scroungers.

Get your guys to schools. Get them the training time they need. Make sure they get sniper training. They are snipers. Demonstrate your team competence to your Command. Get them to come to your trainings. Document the training, and make sure Command knows you are training realistically and what you are capable of accomplishing — and what you can do for them. Go to competitions so you can demonstrate to your team and your Command how you stack up against other teams. The rest of your unit trusts their lives to you. Make sure you're up to the job, and they know you're capable of handling the responsibility.

Don't let Command make them gophers or generalists who do whatever is needed on a mission/call-out. They need to train

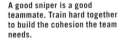

A good sniper is a good teammate. Train hard together to build the cohesion the team needs.

as snipers, prepare for deployment as snipers, and respond as snipers when the mission arises. It's hugely inefficient for your people to wonder whether they are an assaulter or a sniper when the call comes. It takes different gear and a different mindset. It wastes time when they don't know how to train, prepare and deploy because they don't know what they will be doing. Educate your administration that your guys have one focus.

Recognize your limitations regarding training. You can't set up every training session; it's a big job, and you're one person. We rotate training. Every month, another sniper handles training plans. This brings a fresh perspective every training session. I've been doing this for 25 years, and this method ensures that I still get butterflies every training day, wondering what mental and physical challenges the brilliant, masochistic snipers on our team will come up with to challenge and train the rest of us.

Make sure your training is realistic. Shooting groups at 100 yards might be good for your ego, but it's not real life. Shoot under stress, at varied ranges, under physical and mental exertion, with limited time frames, including follow-up shots, on multiple targets, with limited exposure times and target areas, in close proximity to "hostage" targets, around barriers, practicing stalks (with observers trying their darndest to bust you), with land navigation exercises, and, as basic as it sounds, in full gear. If you don't train in your gear, you are cheating yourself.

You have to train like you fight. Make sure your team has their gear set up and usable. That means LBE (Load

Bearing Equipment) and placing the necessary items where the sniper can get to them. If you have your stuff in a pack, what are you going to do when you need it—stop like Santa Claus on a hike and dump out your bag, fumbling through it until you find what you want?

Train past your anticipated needs. Shoot farther than you ever expect to take a shot. Shoot in bad weather, in the dark and in the wind. Shoot under extreme stress. On several occasions, we've sent snipers to medics because they collapsed during training. I've puked in training. It pays off, because I've also puked during a hike-in during a mission.

We have a rule: "Don't ever ask a man to do something on a mission he has not already done in training. Make sure he has done it in training." We have another rule: "Get in shape; stay in shape. The job is tough, the gear is heavy, and no one cares about excuses."

DEPLOY THE TEAM

Once you have a well-trained team that has proven itself to Command, use autonomy. That means you and your sniper team know your job and how to do it,

Communication skills are important, not only between a sniper and their spotter, but between the team and Command as well.

without unnecessary direction from Command. Our team almost never goes to the station for briefing on an incident that's already underway. We respond directly from wherever we are. We set up near the incident and get into position to start relaying information, containing the scene, and protecting the public and the responding team.

Make sure each sniper understands the mission so he can take initiative. Have common procedures so questions are minimized. On-scene, make assignments quickly to get your people deployed in a fashion that gives 360-degree coverage.

Coordinate communications. Make sure you understand communication procedures that work with your entire unit, whether using a common frequency with all responders or having a dedicated sniper frequency due to the huge volume of commo generated by a sniper team.

Consider having a dedicated sniper liaison to compile info for the incident Command. Trying to feed continuous real-time info directly to a commander is like forcing him to drink from a fire hose. It's preferable to transmit the info to a sniper-trained liaison who can collate and provide the info to Command as it's needed.

Make sure you have ROE (Rules of Engagement) procedures in place so every man knows them. Every call-out involves a situation where your team may be required to end someone's life.

Keep track of your guys. Know where they are, what they can see, and what they can do. Know their fields of fire and sectors of fire. Watch to avoid crossfires. Know what they have for concealment and cover. Make sure they have what they need in terms of support, hydration, protection from elements, and communications. Make sure other elements know where they are to avoid conflicts such as moving unknowingly into the team's required field of fire.

Make sure the team is kept up to date on negotiations and movements of other elements. Rotate your guys as needed (and realize they will be reluctant to rotate out). Make sure they are capable of continued performance. If they are outside in −20-degree temperatures, you can't let them stay and freeze to the ground, because they will if you let them. If they are on a black rooftop in 105-degree heat, make sure they get relief to recuperate, hydrate, and cool down.

CONCLUSIONS

Those who know me will tell you I'm an idealist and opinionated. I have opinions on most everything. If you're a team leader — or aspire to be — you may have read some of these points, thinking, *Command will never let me do that* or, *We don't have that degree of control over those things.*

That's not my problem. It's your problem to solve. If you think what I've written makes sense, do what you can to implement what you can, however you can. That's your job as team leader. Do the job in the best, most efficient and safest way you can. And enjoy it.

ANTI-CANT

KEEP YOUR EYE ON THE BUBBLE AND LEVEL YOUR RIFLE FOR EFFECTIVE LONG-RANGE SHOOTING.

By TODD HODNETT

As an instructor of long-range shooting, I have noticed several issues that tend to resurface with each class. One is the problem of a shooter canting his rifle.

Most people will argue that their rifle is not canted, when in reality it is, so the immediate task is to determine whether the reticle is indeed canted. First, purchase a level and properly mount it. Once you have placed a level on your gun and you're at the range, place the reticle on target. Level the reticle to your eye, then check the level for cant to see how well you did. If you were on a flat shooting platform and on a flat range, I would expect that most shooters would do pretty well. However, I've seen more than one shooter surprised at the amount of cant present on a rifle when he felt level at the time.

DEVICES

The first step to correct this problem is to buy a good level for your rifle. There is a large selection of levels available. Some are fairly cheap, while others are rather expensive. Be careful, as some of the models are so nonsensitive that you can cant the level nearly three degrees before the bubble moves. However, I now believe that even a bad level is better than none at all.

Most ranges will have the individual shooting from berm to berm. These berms at each yard line are man-made and fairly flat and level. Also, the trees in the distance behind where we are shooting help us align our reticle with the world. Because we often shoot in flat areas where getting level isn't an issue, it's very confusing when we do find ourselves somewhere where it is hard to determine if we are level. When our rifle is out and we're looking through the reticle, it usually means we're already on the hunt, and then it's too late to figure out if we're canting our scopes.

With an abundance of levels on the market, you need to do a little research before making your purchase. Some of the models available are (in alphabetical order):

Accuracy 1st (accuracy1st.com)
Brownells (brownells.com)
DTAC (davidtubb.com)
Holland (hollandguns.com)
Deros Level Grouse
US Optics (usoptics.com)

Some have unique features such as swivel mounts, covers to protect the vial, top mounts or rail mounts. There are even adjustable features for leveling the bubble while on the rifle and degree markings of cant lines that indicate if you are at 2½, 5, 7½ or 10 degrees.

Any anti-cant device is better than none, but some are definitely better than others. There are a lot of differences in these models. Some mount on the scope, and some mount to the rail.

LEVELING

Once a level is purchased, mount it. The best way to mount a level is to place a colored string and a plumb bob downrange a short distance. It will help if it's not too close, as the string will be blurred because of the inability of the scope to focus at extremely short distances. I'd suggest placing the string and bob between 50 and 100 meters.

Using a bench rest or the prone position, level the scope's vertical stadia to the string. Use colored string to make it easier to see. When you have the vertical stadia aligned perfectly, adjust the anti-cant device to read level. This calibrates the device to your reticle.

If you have a normal-style bubble with a line on each side of it to indicate when the device is level, I suggest adjusting the anti-cant device to where the edge of the bubble is touching one of the lines. This makes it easier to identify when you are exactly level.

Now consider whether you need to make the scope level with the gun. This is something I get asked about in class every week. The real truth is that a lot of competitive shooters will shoot with a cant between the vertical stadia and the vertical line of the rifle stock. I've seen some of my students spend a lot of money on all kinds of levels that they

The level is an integral part of long-range shooting. Without leveling your reticle, it's impossible to know whether your misses are due to botched wind calls or a misaligned reticle.

place all over the rifle and scope. There is nothing wrong with this, but it isn't necessary. You can quickly mount a scope and get it extremely close to level just by using your eye. First, mount the scope as normal, then—once the correct eye relief is adjusted for—pull your eye away from the scope and make the vertical stadia line bisect the buttplate of the stock. After this is done, you can decide if you'd like to have the reticle straight with the rifle's stock line or if you prefer to slightly cant your reticle.

If you do decide to cant your reticle, you'll need to make sure the reticle is still level with your anti-cant device. I would strongly advise against extreme canting of your reticle from the center-ine of your stock. A small cant may allow a more comfortable ergonomic feel between your rifle and shoulder, but too much can destroy the relationship be-tween the centerline axis of your scope and the centerline axis of the bore. This creates external ballistics issues. The most important thing to remember is that you must level the reticle for every shot.

Here we see three different levels available on the market today. When choosing a level, be sure to take into account where the level is placed rela-tive to your field of view and the sensitivity of the level. Some levels allow as much as three degrees of tilt before they show that they're unlevel.

WHY?

I've watched men mistakenly assume that the shot they just missed off the edge of their target was due to some unseen or ill-measured effects of the wind. Deep down, we all realize that we are not as good at calling wind as we would like to be. Winds will always be the nemesis of the long-range shooter. I tell my students that I truly believe every five-mph change equates to a 10 percent loss in first-round-hit capabilities. This applies to targets between 600 to 800 meters with a target size of 12 to 16 inches.

I like to train in an area where winds average 17 mph. The ter-rain features and the cap-rocks that cover the training area also enhance the effects of the wind. Most often, when the shooter barely misses the intended target, he believes that he just narrowly misjudged the wind call. However, a well-trained spotter can (and often does) correct the shooter's cant, and then the shooter can hit the next shot with the exact same wind call.

To show you the math behind shooting a scope that's canted, the following examples show the difference in where the bullet will hit with the cant as opposed to where it would have hit without the cant.

If the scope is canted by only 2½ degrees, the bullet will impact .05 mils for every 100 meters in the direction of the cant.

EXAMPLES:
- A 400-meter shot would have a .2-mil shift (approx. three inches)
- A 600-meter shot would have a .3-mil shift (approx. seven inches)
- An 800-meter shot would have a .4-mil shift (approx. 12 inches)

If the scope is canted five degrees, the bullet will impact .1 mil for every 100 meters in the direction of the cant.

EXAMPLES:
- A 400-meter shot would have a .4-mil shift (approx. six inches)
- A 600-meter shot would have a .6-mil shift (approx. 14 inches)
- An 800-meter shot would have a .8-mil shift (approx. 25 inches)

Most of the time, the shooter will try to level the gun by adjusting the bipod. Even though this would be a proper correction, the shooter may not have the time required for it. By understanding where the bullet will impact due to the cant of the rifle, the shooter can adjust his hold and get the desired impact by holding off the target to account for the impact shift. This takes some training.

Most shooters would think that they could see 2½ degrees and for sure 5 degrees of cant. I would normally agree, until you place a shooter on a downslope and have him shoot at a target on a hillside with the horizon running anywhere but level. This describes all three of the areas in which I take my students for training.

I can understand how shooters on flat ranges without terrain features may not have noticed the problem of not being able to see when their scope was slightly canted. I was fortunate early in my life in that I was running around with a scoped rifle on a daily basis. I had trained my eye to a point that I didn't think I needed help from a level. I know now that I was wrong. Today I want a level on every scope I have.

MULTIPLE SOLUTIONS

So which device should you use? There are many levels available, and most are very affordable. If you really compare anti-cant devices, you will find that some are a lot more accurate than others. Something you may want to consider is where the bubble is placed in relationship to your vision.

The most convenient anti-cant devices allow you to transpose the image of the level onto your reticle. For example, you see the level with your nonshooting eye while you are looking through the scope with your shooting eye. You do this by focusing on the level with your nonshooting eye, then changing focus to your shooting eye, which will drag the image of the level onto the reticle. With a little practice you'll be able to pull the image of the level on demand.

What you don't want to do is lift your head out of the scope to check your level. This is an unnecessary and time-consuming movement. Still, even doing that is much better than not having a level at all. If you can't afford a level, I would suggest that you try looking over the top of the scope and level the top turret to the horizon. This will help solve the canting problem until you can afford to purchase a level.

Take time to learn the differences in the products you're looking into. Pick a quality level, and better enjoy your time on the range and improve your long-range shooting.

TEMPERATURE EFFECT

Photo courtesy of US Army

HOW LITTLE THE OLD RULE ACTUALLY APPLIES TO ACCURACY WITHIN 500 YARDS.

BY JEFF HOFFMAN

'For every 20 degrees of temperature change, adjust one MOA to compensate for the ballistics change." Everyone who has ever heard that in a sniper school, please raise your hand.

It must be true, because it's printed in the U.S. Army sniper manual and spoken in nearly every basic sniper school in the country. Those of you who know me know that I'll tell you it's B.S. Actually, it is technically true, but only at such far distances that they exceed any recorded law enforcement sniper shot ever made. This rule is dangerous because it tells police snipers

to start changing their sights when it's not necessary. Doing so leads you away from the correct firing solution. The problem is that it has been taught for so long now that it has nearly become sniping gospel. This rule continues to be repeated and accepted despite the fact that it is so easily proved wrong by testing in the field under a variety of temperatures. As snipers, isn't that what we are supposed to do? Shoot under a variety of circumstances and carefully note the results? Bad information can lead to bad results.

Sniper instructor John Simpson has a great saying: "If you can't show me the math, then it's just your opinion." I can show you the math. After that, it's up to you to go to the field and verify with your rifle what I am about to explain.

There are two factors to temperature effect: internal ballistics and external ballistics. Internal ballistics is what happens within the gun. So the question is, how does the temperature of the propellant affect its rate of combustion and thus projectile velocity? Answer: Typically, higher temperatures cause the powder to burn faster, generating more pressure and velocity. External ballistics is what happens to the projectile during its flight upon exiting the muzzle to the target. Which takes us to our second question: How does the temperature of the air affect the flight of the bullet? Answer: Cold air is denser than warm air. Cold air thus provides more drag on the bullet and causes it to lose velocity more quickly. As the bullet slows, it drops more quickly; that is a bullet's vertical drop relative to the distance traveled.

The problem we face is that while the manual is technically correct at long distances, law enforcement sniping usually takes place at between zero and 200 yards. Even most military shots are made within 500 yards, so those wearing a military uniform should pay attention as well.

THE NEW RULE
I will make a bold statement here that makes everything pretty simple to calculate. Here's the new rule: For sniping to 500 yards, ignore temperature effect. With that gauntlet thrown down, here's the math.

INTERNAL BALLISTIC EFFECT
With a .308 Win. cartridge, you can generally assume that for every degree of temperature change, you can expect approximately one to 1½ fps in velocity change. I can show the test results behind the generalization if anyone wants to see them. Let's look at what effect we might experience. To keep the math simple, let's work with the 20-degree change that the sniper manual mentions. That easily translates to a velocity effect of 20 to 30 fps.

You should note that there are modern, temperature-insensitive powders available that essentially eliminate even that change. My company, Black Hills Ammunition, uses these new propellants in our .308 Win. and 7.62x51 NATO 175-grain loads, and we are moving it to other .308-caliber loads, but for the purposes of this article, let's assume that the 20 to 30 fps variation still exists.

Decreasing the starting velocity from 2,650 fps to 2,620 fps at sea level with a 168-grain BTHP match bullet results in an added drop of 1.7 inches at 500 yards. Remember this, because we will now check the external ballistic effect, then combine the two effects to see what the total effect actually is.

EXTERNAL BALLISTIC EFFECT
The difference in air density resulting in a change from 80 to 60 degrees amounts to a bullet-drop difference of .9 inch at 500 yards. The combined internal and external ballistic effect of a 20-degree temperature change is 2.6 inches at 500 yards, approximately half MOA.

The "one MOA per 20 degrees of temperature" rule does not become true until 700 yards, even when combining the internal and external ballistic effect. The variation may be half MOA at 500 yards, but it's less than that and absolutely insignificant at the more common law enforcement engagement distances of 200 yards or less. The effect is less than the change in point of impact that you can induce by changing body position or failing to adjust your parallax. I submit to you that it is so insignificant, you should ignore it altogether.

SPEED AND PRECISION
I realize that our business as snipers is to be precise, but it's also to be fast. If you spend time diddling with insignificant variables while you should be concentrating on the more important factors, you'll lose the race. The important factors after evaluating and deciding whether to even use deadly force are range to the target, wind effect and required leads. If you spend time calculating, then apply an inappropriate rule, the result is worse than the wasted time. It can mean a miss.

Even an extreme swing of 80 degrees will only result in a maximum of a half-MOA point of impact change at 200 yards compared with the four-MOA shift that would be predicted by the often-repeated rule of "one MOA adjustment for

every 20 degrees of temperature change." If you apply the "20 degree" rule to a 200-yard shot in this circumstance, the result is a miss by seven inches.

That's the math. Want real-world results? I am a law enforcement sniper in South Dakota. I have shot in extremes from 30 degrees below zero to 110. I average around 1,600 rounds per year recorded through my .308-caliber sniper rifle. I have steel ranges set up and waiting for me any time I want to go shoot. I regularly train to 600 yards, in all temperatures. My observations in the field verify the computer solution. Out to 500 yards, I ignore the temperature. Take the time to verify temperature effect for yourself.

Many times we experience a small variation in our zero from the last time we shot, and as reasoning snipers we try to explain it. I do it, too. We have an obligation to ourselves to ask those questions. I can tell you, however, that when it happens at ranges of less than 500 yards, the math won't back where up the conclusion that temperature-induced internal or external ballistic variations are significant factors. Keep looking in another area. Hint: It won't be humidity, altitude or barometric pressure. These are variables best covered in another article.

45°

HIGH ANGLES

THE BULLET DOESN'T LIE.

BY TODD HODNETT

It is amazing the misconceptions shooters have about shooting angle fire. I think this is due to the fact that most have never shot high angles because true high-angle fire is extremely hard to find in the U.S. Don't misunderstand me: I am talking about high-angle fire, not angle fire. Most of the misconceptions out there are based on things heard or read by the shooter, because he has never had the opportunity to engage targets where the inclination represents high-angle fire. I am going to show you a couple of high-angle formulas I have developed that make this type of shooting simple.

One should understand that a lot of the formulas out there are not correct. My formulas are built around where the bullet hits. The bullet can't talk, so it cannot tell a lie. What I do is build formulas that replicate the actual performance of the flight path of the bullet.

The key to this is that you have to shoot it. This is where I'm lucky; I have a high-angle facility near Monument Valley where I live. I can get true high-angle fire, not just slight angles.

One of the first misconceptions a shooter will have to address is the perception of angle. Most people will think the angle is much greater than it is. Several people have told me that they have shot at 45 degrees or greater, but when they actually measure the angle, they find it is not even 30 degrees. It really did look steep. I have been at ranges where the steepest target was only 30 degrees at 300 meters. This shot would only require an adjusted hold of 3½ inches. Not much of a needed adjustment. So the perception of angle must be dealt with first, and there are several devices that work great. Here are a few.

Angle indicators are one method of verifying the angle of the shot. While accurate, it is one more piece of gear that needs to be carried and can get lost.

I will show you a solution that is free and works pretty well. The men I train at Accuracy 1st are going through doors and/or jumping out of helicopters, so life can be pretty rough on their weapon systems. I came up with a tool that can't be broken or lost. You will need a tool that will measure angles, like a protractor, iPhone or something similar. Place that on your gun and tilt the gun until the device indicates 30 degrees. At this time you will need to place a mark on your stock with the use of a "plumb bob" (a weight with a string). Then repeat this procedure at 45 degrees and 60 degrees, with both up angles and down angles placed on the stock. I am having a sticker made that has the angles marked on it so guys can just make sure the top line is level with the barrel and peel off the back and stick it on the stock. Simple, yet effective.

When you shoot angle-fire shots, all you need to do is look at the target in your scope and then look at what line is pointing straight to the ground, thus giving you the angle for the shot. You can place as many marks as you desire, but I have found that these three angles are enough

for me. The reason is that 60 degrees at any distance—and distance is the key—is extremely hard to find, and angle fire of 15 degrees, which can be found anywhere, doesn't really matter. You are looking at only around .22 mils difference in impact, or 5.2 inches at 600 meters. Plus, it is easy to do the math at 15 degrees, but I don't have to have it marked, I can see if it is halfway between zero and 30 degrees.

I am not going into what I think of the Pythagorean theorem. What I can say is that it takes too

long even if it gives correct holds at distance. The reality is that we need a quick firing solution that we can do in our head—one that gives us the results we want. So let's get into the formulas.

THREE EASY RULES:

- 30 degrees = subtract half-MOA or .15 mil every 100m from your normal hold
- 45 degrees = subtract 1 MOA or .3 mil every 100m from your normal hold

The extreme angle shown in the photo to the left will need to be taken into account for an effective shot. The soldier shooting above will require much less correction.

- 60 degrees = subtract 2 MOA or .6 mil every 100m from your normal hold and then add 1 MOA or .3 mil back to the hold

(This formula works really well for .308 rifles.)

So let's work through some examples.

Take a distance of 500 meters and apply all three angles, showing the math.

The gun we will be showing in the examples is a .308 with a muzzle velocity of 2,600 fps and BC of .475. The atmospherics will be 27.0 and 70 degrees.

The 500 meters distance has a dope of 3.6 mils, or 12.4 MOA.

So for 30 degrees I would take 3.6 mils and subtract 2.5 MOA (half MOA x 5) or .75 mil for an answer of 2.85 mils; the real answer is 2.9 mils.

Let's try 45 degrees. Take the 3.6 and subtract 5 MOA (1 MOA x 5) or 1.5 mils for an answer of 2.1 mils; the actual answer is 2.07 mils.

Now 60 degrees. We take 3.6 and subtract 9 MOA (2 MOA x 5, then add 1 back) or 2.7 mils, and you get an answer of .9 mil, and the real answer is .99 mil.

So as you can see, this is a very simple formula that anyone can do in his head.

You may find yourself with MOA scope adjustments with BDC calibrated marks on the turret. Those scopes are still out there, but I hope we are moving out of the era of MOA turrets with BDCs and mil reticles combined. This makes no sense, and as people gain knowledge, they are moving to a mil/mil system. I am not against having a BDC along with the mils, but it has to be done right, and most scopes are wrong for the "600 meters and beyond"

BDC marks with corrected DA. It wasn't Leupold's fault that the military asked for these types of turrets. This was the requirement at the time.

If you find yourself with this type of scope, with half-MOA adjustments on the turret, this is how I would use it.

Shooting at a target at 500 meters, dial 5 on the BDC, then take off 5 clicks of elevation for a 30-degree angle shot.

Example math: For a target with 45 degrees at the same range you would take off 10 clicks (half-MOA x 10 = 5 MOA).

For a target off 60 degrees, you would take off 12 MOA and then add one back, meaning you would dial to the 6 on the BDC and then take off 11 MOA, or 22 clicks on a half-MOA turret.

So simple and without having to think about math, these

results show close corrected elevation holds to what the ballistic solver shows. These results are also proven time and again in training.

When I begin a high-angle class, I have the student shoot his normal dope for the range of the target without inclination plugged in. This will allow the student to gain knowledge of how much deviation he can expect for the effects of an angle shot. Then we move into using the ballistic solver to give us a corrected hold for inclination in which the student can see how accurate the ballistic solver truly is. After that we move into the speed formulas, allowing the student to use my formulas to get fast, accurate holds that he can do in his head. Whether you are a hunter, military or LE shooter, a fast, accurate hold can be very important. I always tell my students that if they have time, the ballistic solver is very

Angle shooting, by nature, usually implies shooting from unconventional and precarious positions. The less complicated we can make our lives in moments like these, the easier it will be to make our shots.

accurate and the choice to use. Nevertheless, my formulas allow the shooter to get a correct hold that is very close to the mathematical corrected holds the ballistic solver uses.

If you are not shooting a .308, here is another formula that I came up with several years ago. This formula is made for mil turret/mil reticle scopes.

To make the math simple, this formula uses the sine instead of the cosine for the angle. In the result, you will see that from the sine, we are able to obtain the cosine through simple third-grade math.

RULES

- 30 degrees = subtract 10 percent of the hold, then subtract .15 mil from the total

- 45 degrees = subtract 30 percent of the hold, then subtract .5 mil from the total

- 60 degrees = subtract 50 percent of the hold, then subtract .75 mil from the total

EXAMPLES

- 600m hold of 4.97 mils

- 30 degree = 5 mils – .5 (10 percent) = 4.5, then subtract .15 mil for a total of 4.35 mils

- Ballistic solver answer is 4.1 mils

- 45 degree = 5 mils – 1.5 mils (30 percent) = 3.5 mils – .5 mil = 3 mils

- Ballistic solver answer is 3.04 mils.

- 60 degree = 5 mils – 2.5 mils = 2.5 mils – .75 mil = 1.75 mils

- Ballistic solver answer is 1.67 mils.

Now you're probably wondering where the .15, .5, .75 mil come from. We are subtracting the sine of the constant, which is 1.5 mils.

The reason this is so simple is that we are taking a number that you know as your dope if you memorized your range card, or if you haven't memorized it, you have attached it to your gun somewhere. Then we just work off the cosine or sine of the angle, depending on how you want to look at it·

The ballistic solver is an awesome tool for this, and that is why we put the high-angle chart on the back of the Accuracy 1st Whiz Wheel. Just line up the flat distance dope with the angle— no math needed.

Remember that high-angle shooting is very rarely done in the prone, so real-angle fire is a class in unconventional positional shooting.

And remember that not all angle fire formulas will work at true angle fire where the range is far enough and the angle steep enough. So the best way to know for sure is to get out and shoot it. But don't be intimidated. Angle fire is easy—so easy that I try to get my students back to Texas to train in the high winds with terrain features that we get around the caprocks. You will always need more time learning winds, as this is where 90 percent of all misses originate. Wind is the No. 1 reason we miss shots in long-range shooting, and

this includes high-angle fire. Even though you may be taking a shot at 600 meters with a 60-degree down angle, you may be using a rangefinder that corrects for angle distance. If it shows 300 meters, you are still doing a wind formula for the full 600 meters.

In conclusion, angle fire makes a difference if you shoot at a target with real angles and enough distance. Most places won't give you both. They may have something that looks steep, but it is not high angle and may not be enough of an angle to make you miss your target with your normal dope.

We shoot high angle in Utah, but I also go to the Palo Duro canyon in Texas, which is the second largest canyon in the U.S. Here we have only angle fire and show that it doesn't matter. There is not enough angle and distance combined to give us a real need to adjust our hold. The purpose of this is to show when angle fire matters and when it doesn't. Be smart and make the most of your training time. High angle is fun, not hard.

INVIS

INFLUENCE

A WIND FORMULA YOU CAN ACTUALLY USE IN THE FIELD.

BY JEFF HOFFMAN

IBLE

A critical component of shooting accurately in the wind is accurately measuring wind speed. A Kestrel handheld weather station accomplishes this task magnificently.

PHOTO BY DoD

A sniper needs to accurately measure, then compensate for, wind. He needs a formula to calculate wind effect that is easily remembered and can be utilized quickly in the field without looking at charts or using a calculator.

Someone once said, "The amateur is concerned with trajectory. The professional is concerned with wind effect." He's right. Trajectory is relatively predictable because gravity doesn't change. Wind effect changes not only with range, but also with the velocity of the wind and the angle relative to the path of the bullet.

To be effective at long range, a sniper needs to be able to accurately predict and compensate for the effect of prevailing wind upon his bullet. To do this he needs a formula for accurately calculating the wind effect that is easily remembered and can be utilized quickly in the field without looking at charts or using a calculator. There is a standard U.S. military formula that all serious snipers have seen. I won't go into details over it except to say that I can't use it in the field, and I have heard the same from snipers on the most skilled and respected teams in the world. It is simply too difficult to complete without a calculator.

A few years ago a fellow law enforcement sniper and I entered a competition held for both police and military snipers. As police snipers we did well out to 400 yards, but at longer distances we had our butts handed to us by military snipers who had more experience shooting in wind. Humility is a great motivator, so when I got back, I had steel targets made and started shooting long range in the wind. I also sat in front of a computer screen with a ballistics program and studied the trajectory and effect of wind on a .308 match projectile at various ranges.

My goal was to find a simplified formula that could be used in the field, quickly and while under stress. The formula I came up with is relatively quick, uses very basic math and is easily remembered and used in the field without resorting to charts, notes and calculators.

Three Basic Steps

This formula provides the firing solution in terms of minutes of

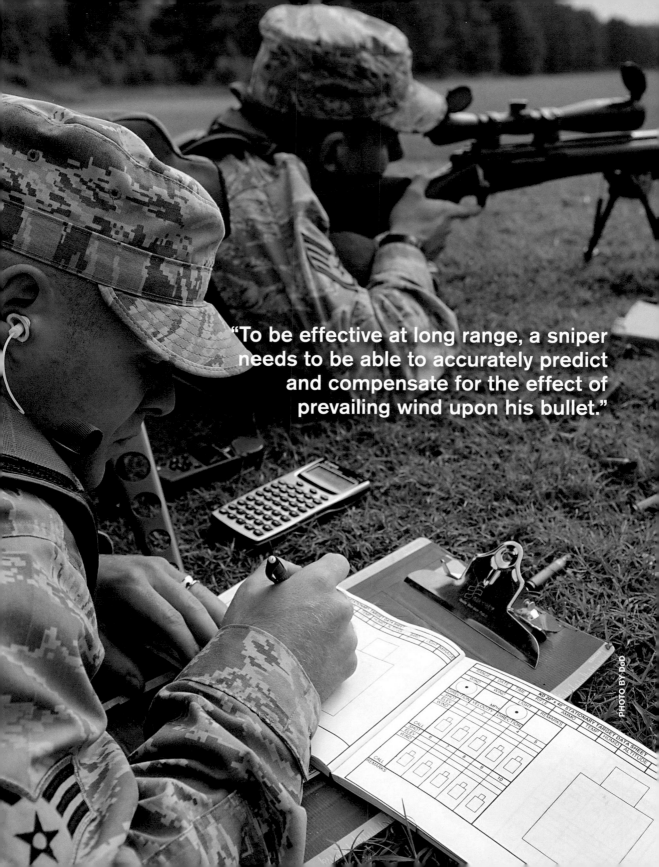

"To be effective at long range, a sniper needs to be able to accurately predict and compensate for the effect of prevailing wind upon his bullet."

angle (MOA) and is for the .308 Match and 7.62x51 NATO sniping rounds, such as M118LR. It allows you to either dial in the correction or hold off using Mil-Dot spaces as reference.

IT HAS THREE BASIC STEPS:

1. Make your initial calculation based on a 10-mph full-value wind.
2. Adjust for actual wind speed.
3. Adjust for actual wind value.

You can't accurately compensate for wind effect unless you can accurately estimate wind speed. For this, you need an accurate wind gauge. I highly recommend the basic Kestrel-brand unit, the Kestrel 1000. You should practice with it to the point that you can reliably feel and observe wind in field conditions and know what the actual wind velocity is based on your observations. With practice, you will be able to call wind speed accurately without use of the wind gauge. This is important because our goal is to be fast and accurate, without any crutches. Your target won't wait while you are

PHOTO BY DoD

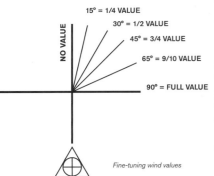

Fine-tuning wind values

digging for stuff to help with your calculations.

The Formula

The formula I came up with is:

Range (in yards, expressed as a single digit) − 1 = x MOA of correction needed (based on a 10-mph full-value wind).

Example: If you intend to hit a target 700 yards away, you would need to allow 6 minutes of wind correction: 7-1= 6. If you had an 800-yard target, you would need 7 minutes of correction: 8-1=7. If you had a 500-yard target you would need 4 minutes of correction: 5-1=4.

That's the first step, again, regardless of actual existing wind speed or value. Next, you need to adjust for actual wind speed and actual wind value. It makes no difference in which order you do the next two steps.

Acual Wind Speed

Wind will deflect the bullet in direct proportion to the speed of the wind. A 20-mph wind affects the bullet exactly twice as much as a 10-mph wind. A 5-mph wind will deflect the bullet one-half as much as a 10-mph wind. A 15-mph wind will deflect the bullet 50 percent more than a 10-mph wind. This makes it easy for us to use the basic formula and alter it to be accurate under conditions where the wind is something other than 10 mph.

Example: You are shooting at a target 700 yards away with a 5-mph, full-value wind. Do the basic formula: 7-1=6 MOA of correction. Because you are shooting in a 5-mph wind, not a 10-mph wind, adjust your calculation by cutting the estimated wind deflection by one half: 6÷2=3 MOA of correction needed.

I put wind into increments of 3, 5, 7, 10, 15 and 20. I like 3 as correction because I have a tough time remembering all the wind-speed indicators, such as leaves blowing and trees swaying, but I know that if I can feel a wind on my face, it is worth at least a 3-mph compensation.

One way of compensating for winds that are a fraction of the basic 10-mph wind is to take your initial calculation made for a 10-mph wind and multiply it by .3, .7, etc. If our target is 700 yards away, with a 3-mph wind, the calculation might look like this: 7-1=6, 6x.3=1.8 MOA of correction needed. Scopes don't allow for an exact 1.8 MOA correction, so we dial in 1.75 MOA, 2 MOA or hold off one-half mil. All will result in a hit.

Actual Wind Value

The formula we are using here is based (for the initial calculation) on a full-value wind. Not all winds are full value. For the last step we need to adjust for the actual wind value. Many sniper schools teach only three wind values: full value (a wind perpendicular to the path of the bullet), no value (running the same angle as the path of the bullet, either straight to you or straight away from you) and half value. They teach that everything between full and no value is half value. This is too rough for my taste. It may put you on a human-size target out to 600 yards, but to hit past that or to hit with more precision, you should break it down more precisely. More

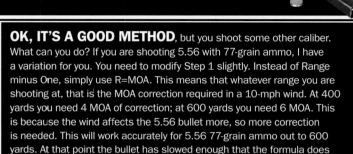

OTHER CALIBERS

OK, IT'S A GOOD METHOD, but you shoot some other caliber. What can you do? If you are shooting 5.56 with 77-grain ammo, I have a variation for you. You need to modify Step 1 slightly. Instead of Range minus One, simply use R=MOA. This means that whatever range you are shooting at, that is the MOA correction required in a 10-mph wind. At 400 yards you need 4 MOA of correction; at 600 yards you need 6 MOA. This is because the wind affects the 5.56 bullet more, so more correction is needed. This will work accurately for 5.56 77-grain ammo out to 600 yards. At that point the bullet has slowed enough that the formula does not give sufficient correction.

I have determined that this formula can also be used for other calibers by applying a correction factor. A .300 Win. Mag. with a 190-grain Match bullet is affected only 70 percent as much as a .308 175-grain bullet. You can do the calculations as a final Step 4: multiply by .7 to adjust for the lesser wind drift of the .300 Win. Mag. projectile. Similarly, a .338 Lapua has a .6 correction factor, and a .50 BMG has a .4 correction factor.

important, a primary assumption of this teaching is wrong. A perfect 45-degree wind has a three-quarter value, not a half-value, as most schools teach. (A

45-degree wind actually has a true effect of .707, so you can do the math by using three-quarters of your calculation to this point, or you can make the math a little easier and multiply by .7, which is what I do.) A 30-degree wind is a true half value.

So how do we use actual wind value? You need to take the result of your calculation up to this point and adjust it for actual wind value. Let's put it all together.

Example: Assume you have a target at 700 yards with a 5-mph wind, intersecting the line from you to the target at a 45-degree angle. What is the correction needed?

Step 1: Since the target is at 700, we know we need 6 MOA of correction for Step 1 (7-1=6).

Step 2: It's a 5-mph wind, so we cut that number in half to get 3 MOA (6÷2=3).

Step 3: Because the wind is at 45 degrees, we need to multiply the 3 MOA by .7 to get 2.1.

We use .7 because a 45-degree wind affects the bullet only 70 percent of what it would if it were a perfect full-value wind: 3x.7=2.1. Obviously, we round this to 2 MOA of correction needed.

Tips

This formula is caliber-specific for .308 175-grain Match or 7.62 M118LR. It works well for .308 168-grain Match, but the 168-grain Match is an inferior choice for distances past 600 yards.

Not all targets you are presented with are at even 100-yard increments. I round down to a great extent, because the formula tends to err slightly toward overstating wind effect. If the target were at 735 yards, for wind-calculation purposes I would call it 700 and my first calculation would result in 6 MOA of needed wind correction.

The formula is based on normal atmospheric conditions: sea level to 4,000 feet elevation and, say, zero to 90 degrees F. If you are higher in elevation than that or hotter than that in temperature, the air will be thinner, resulting in less wind deflection. The solution is to change the initial calculation to R-2=x MOA of correction, rather than R-1=x MOA of correction, and proceed from there in the same manner as previously described.

Wind at the shooter's location may not be the same as that at the target or at any point in between. I normally estimate it at my shooting position, then look along the path to the target for indications of wind. What are the grass, trees and dust doing? What is the mirage doing? What is the terrain along the path? Does the terrain block the wind at some points, or is it likely that the wind is being funneled through at a higher velocity than what I am feeling?

It is important when determining wind angle to try to be precise in your estimate. I don't simply face the target when determining wind angle. I draw an imaginary line between the target and me. I then try to determine the angle at which the wind intersects that line.

Practice with the Formula

Any formula is useless unless you can apply it. You have to practice using it in order to be fast enough to do the math in your head, while under pressure, before the conditions change. You also have to develop the confidence in knowing that it works for you by actually using it in the field.

Spend the money and buy a good wind gauge. If you don't, you're wasting your time because you can't apply the formula unless you know the wind speed. Being able to estimate wind speed comes from practice in the field with the wind gauge.

Remember, wind problems are tough to solve perfectly. If you somehow were able to solve it perfectly, by the time you calculated your answer, the problem would be different because your target would have moved or the wind would have changed in strength or angle. Speed of calculation with a reasonably accurate method is far superior to a perfect answer that arrives too late. You have to be willing to accept some estimation error and some rounding in the interest of speed.

DISTANCE SHOOTING FOR POLICE

A PRIMER ON APPLYING ELEVATION AND WINDAGE ADJUSTMENTS.

BY JEFF HOFFMAN

"**L**ong range" is a relative term. For purposes of this lesson on law enforcement sniping, we will discuss ranges between zero and 600 yards. No shot in history made by a law enforcement officer has exceeded 500 yards. A law enforcement sniper has to take into account means, opportunity and jeopardy when making lethal-force decisions, so we must be able to articulate why a shot is even necessary at

unusual distances. We also have to be absolutely certain of target identification. With those things in mind, we can begin to discuss how to hit at those ranges. I will assume that all students to this lesson fully understand operation of their rifle, including how to make scope adjustments for elevation and windage.

There are two primary elements to hitting a distant target: elevation and windage.

They are influenced by the major factors in shooting, to include the effect of gravity and drag of the air on the bullet, which causes it to slow and drop as it travels downrange. At the same time, the effect of wind pushes the projectile off of a straight course as the bullet travels farther at a continually slowing velocity. Let's take these elements one at a time, starting with elevation.

ELEVATION

Elevation requires compensating for the trajectory of the projectile as it travels downrange. This is the easy part of the problem, because as you will learn, trajectory is a relatively predictable factor. It will do very nearly the same thing for every shot. Trajectory is primarily influenced by the efficiency of the bullet moving through the air (known technically as its BC, or ballistic coefficient) and the starting velocity of the bullet. Both of these things are known to a pretty high degree of precision, so the biggest variable in calculating trajectory is range. Think of it this way: "Where do I have to hold, or how much do I have to compensate to make sure the projectile strikes the distant target as the bullet is being pulled to the earth?"

There are several ways to get the answer without having to do complicated math. There are a number of ballistic calculators out there and many sources for ballistic dope cards. But the very best way to figure how your rifle behaves is to take your rifle and ammunition to a range and actually shoot at the distances you need to know the dope for. Then record your results. This gives you actual versus predicted results and is the information you need to rely on. There are many small variables in predicted data, but even so, dope cards and ballistic printouts are usually very close and can get you on target while you refine the actual data for your own rifle.

There are two ways to adjust for the curved trajectory of the projectile as it travels: hold off and dialing the dope. Let's start by assuming a zero of 100 yards with your rifle. This means that the bullet exits the muzzle of your

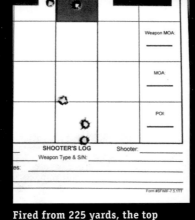

Fired from 225 yards, the top group in the center of this target represents a dope that was dialed in after the lower group was shot. The author recommends that an LE sniper dial in his dope for targets beyond 125 yards rather than holding off with the reticle.

rifle approximately two inches below your line of sight, i.e. where your crosshairs indicate.

The scope is adjusted so that the point at the center of the crosshairs and the fired projectile will converge at 100 yards. The muzzle of the rifle is actually pointed at a slight upward angle compared with the line of sight in order for the bullet to impact the target. At very close distances, the point of impact will thus be nearly two inches below the crosshairs. At 25 yards, the bullet will have risen to be only about .6 inch below the crosshair. At 50 and 75 yards, the bullet will be so close to your point of aim, it's not worth adjusting for. The point of impact will coincide with the point indicated by the crosshair at 100 yards. At 125 yards, you will be about a half inch low, or approximately half MOA, as the bullet drops due to gravity, and about 1.3 inches low, or approximately .75 MOA, at 150 yards. For these distances you may decide not to dial any adjustment and just allow for the strike of the bullet. Personally, I hold off at ranges to about 125 yards and then start dialing in adjustments to compensate for trajectory changes beyond that. If the shooter is in a static position, beyond 125 yards I recommend that a law enforcement sniper dial the scope to adjust for the path of the bullet.

For ranges greater than this, I recommend that a sniper memorize the dope in increments of 100 yards from 100 to 600 yards. "Why should I do that," you say, "when I have a nifty little dope card that tells me what adjustments to make?" The dope card is a crutch, a backup plan, a training aid. In a real situation it will likely be dark, and the card will be lost or in the back pocket of your BDUs. The situation will be unfolding so rapidly that you'll need to know the solution

To make good wind calls, you need to consider wind speed, angle and distance to the target. As distance increases, the necessary corrections increase dramatically. Both targets were fired in wind of 7 to 10 mph, blowing full value from the right. At 200 yards the point of impact was only slighly left, with no correction dialed in. At 700 yards, this group is nicely centered, but it required six MOA of correction. That amounts to over 42 inches of wind drift.

without having to look at the card. If you memorize the calculations needed for a 200-, 300-, 400-, 500- and 600-yard shot, you'll have the answer available almost immediately. For distances between these numbers, simply interpolate from the known range to get the answer. Your dope might look like this:

Range/MOA Correction
100 yd.—0 MOA
200 yd.— 2 MOA
300 yd.—5 MOA
400 yd.—8 MOA
500 yd.—12 MOA
600 yd.—16 MOA

I also suggest that you write or tape this simplified information to the side of your stock. We move now to the toughest external variable, wind.

WINDAGE
Adjusting for wind is tougher than adjusting for range, because wind is not constant. It varies in speed and angle, changes from one moment to the next and increases in effect as distance to the target increases and the bullet slows. You have to be mindful that terrain may affect wind. You may feel no wind at your position, but it might be gusting 15 or 20 miles per hour at the target. It's impossible to make a perfect wind call, because by the time you get it calculated perfectly, the situation has probably changed. What's important is to make a fast and accurate assessment of the current wind and its estimated effect in order to get the shot off before conditions change.

How can you do this? The first step is to purchase a wind gauge. I like the Kestrel brand. It's relatively inexpensive, compact and accurate. You cannot calculate for a given wind speed unless you know what the wind speed is. Practice with the wind gauge the same way you train with a radar unit. Guess the speed, then check your guess against the gauge. You'll become good at estimating wind speed quickly if you practice. Other traditional methods such as watching flags, the movement of grass, the mirage, smoke and blown items are also good, but they're best used in conjunction with the gauge and perceptual experience in judging the wind by feel.

Let's now assume that you can determine the wind speed. Remember that you are measuring the wind speed at your location only, while in real time the wind influences a fired bullet the entire course toward the target. The military has a formula for wind effect, but I won't teach it here because no law enforcement sniper actually uses it outside of sniper school. It's just too complicated. I'll teach you a method here that's much easier, doesn't require a

FIGURE 1

Problem: A 500-yard shot with a 10-mph full-value wind

Solution: 4 MOA

Math: 5-1 = 4 MOA

Explanation: The wind is 10 mph and full value, so no further math is needed.

FIGURE 2

Problem: A 500-yard shot with a five-mph full-value wind

Solution: 2 MOA

Math: 5-1 = 4 MOA, then 4 MOA/2 = 2 MOA

Explanation: Because the wind is five mph and not 10 mph, you must divide your base answer by two to get the answer of two MOA.

FIGURE 3

Problem: A 500-yard shot with a five-mph, half-value wind

Solution: 1 MOA

Math: 5-1 = 4 MOA, then 4 MOA/2 = 2 MOA, then 2 MOA/2 = 1 MOA

Explanation: You must further reduce the answer because it is a half-value wind, 2 MOA/2 = 1 MOA.

This is the simplest method I have found. With practice it is very fast, and it is accurate to within a half minute at 1,000 yards.

calculator and can be done in the field while you're actively looking through the riflescope.

BLACK HILLS "RANGE MINUS ONE" FORMULA

This method has three steps. It bases all calculations on the effect that a 10-mph wind will have on a .308-caliber bullet traveling at any given range. Once you know the range, a very simple calculation provides a solution to compensate for the effect of a 10-mph wind at range. You then make two adjustments to the base calculation: Adjust

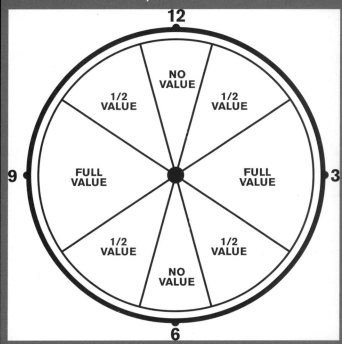

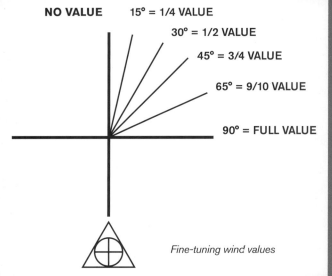

Fine-tuning wind values

Illustration courtesy of Maj. John L. Plaster, USAR (ret.)

Shown at top is a simplified wind diagram used in basic sniper schools. This diagram is sufficient for LE sniping distances due to the shorter distances typical for LE sniping and the need for fast calculations. The chart beneath it is more detailed and accurate. The finer detail of the bottom chart becomes important to the sniper as the range increases. One clarification should be made to what has been often incorrectly taught in basic sniper schools. A true "half-value" wind is actually a 30-degree wind. A 45-degree wind actually has a .7 value, as correctly shown on the more detailed chart on the bottom.

for the actual wind speed, because all winds are not 10-mph winds, and adjust for the wind value based on its angle in relation to the direction of the shot you are about to take.

The base formula for determining the wind effect on a .308-caliber bullet is this:

Range (expressed in hundreds of yards) minus one equals the MOA of correction necessary for a 10-mph wind at that range. As an example, for a 500-yard shot in a 10-mph wind, you need four MOA of wind correction (5-1=4). It is that easy. For a 300-yard shot in the same conditions, you need two MOA (3-1=2).

You now need to adjust for actual wind speed. Wind will move the bullet away from its flight path an amount directly proportional to the speed of the wind. A five-mph wind has half the effect of a 10-mph wind. A 15-mph wind will have a 50 percent added effect. A 20-mph wind will have double the effect. Simply adjust your base calculation accordingly. This formula works between 200 and 1,000 yards. At 100 yards, a 10-mph full-value wind will blow a typical .308 sniping projectile about .7 inch. Use that information rather than the formula for shots of 100 yards or less. For ranges between 100-yard range increments, round to the nearest 100 yards.

The last factor is wind angle. A full-value wind is a wind that is blowing at 90 degrees to the path of the bullet. It will have the most effect. A wind that is blowing perfectly along the path of the bullet, either with the bullet or against the bullet, will not blow the bullet sideways. It is called a no-value wind. A wind that is blowing at a 30-degree angle off the path of the bullet is a half-value wind. Many sniper schools do not break down wind calling past those three calls. They lump everything that's not full value or no value into a half-value category. This might be accurate enough for short-range shooting, which almost all LE shooting is, but understand that it is a generalization used for speed and simplicity, and a more precise examination of the wind angle will provide better precision needed for longer-range targets. Let's go with these three values for now and give some examples of how to use the formula (Figure 1, 2 and 3).

This has been a quick briefing on how to accurately shoot at long distance. To successfully demonstrate what you have learned, you must:

Determine the range.

Calculate the elevation correction needed for that range and apply that correction.

Determine the wind speed.

Calculate the effect the wind will have, using the formula provided, and apply that correction.

Make the shot before the conditions change.

Your goal should be to perform these calculations in the field from memory and make hits quickly. Situations can change quickly, and you have a huge advantage if you can do the mental calculations without the need of calculators, note cards, pens, papers or smart phones.

STUMBLIN' AND BUMBLIN'

LAND NAVIGATION REALLY ISN'T WITCHCRAFT, EVEN WHEN DONE AT NIGHT.

BY TOM BECKSTRAND

If we make it a habit to be outdoors, the ability to navigate becomes essential. Every year, hikers and hunters get lost in the woods, and sometimes this mistake is fatal. Exacerbating the problem is the fact that there are few places that teach land navigation. REI teaches courses on the subject if you happen to live near one of their larger stores. One of the best free resources available for learning land navigation is the Army's Field Manual (FM) devoted to the subject. If you Google "FM 3-25.26," you can find it in PDF form and download it for a reference.

As opposed to covering the basics of land navigation (which we don't have the space for here), we're going to look at some tips and tricks we've learned after practicing the skill for a few years. We can't stress enough the importance of gaining a solid understanding of the basics. Once we know these well, we can begin to implement some of the more advanced techniques that can save us time and effort.

TERRAIN ASSOCIATION IS YOUR BFF

Terrain association is the ability to connect the terrain we see with our eyes with what our map displays. It works well in places with significant terrain relief, such as mountains, valleys and rivers.

A good way to visualize and remind ourselves of terrain features is to make a fist with our palm facing down. Our fist just became a mountain range, and each one of our knuckles is a hilltop. All four of our knuckles together are a ridgeline. The depression between each knuckle is a saddle. Our fingers represent spurs as they descend away from our knuckle, or the "hilltop." The gaps, or low ground, between our fingers are draws. The smooth side of our fist is a cliff.

It's important to know each terrain feature and what it looks like. It is vital to be able to identify each on a map as well. Ridgelines and spurs are the best places to move, as they afford rapid movement and are often sparsely vegetated. Draws are our arch enemies and must be confronted with great care. We must never enter a draw at night, as it will likely be daylight before we exit.

Another easy visual aid is to cup our hand to help distinguish between a valley and a depression. The gaps between our fingers are valleys and will drain if we try to fill them with water, just like real valleys do. Our palm represents a depression and does not drain.

Valleys can give us a way to move quickly if they are wide enough to be flat on the bottom. Depressions are never a good idea, as they hold water and often have thick vegetation. Sometimes we call those swamps, and swamps are places of profound and abiding difficulty for those trying to navigate.

Once we learn to identify each feature on the map and correlate it with the terrain in front of us, we're ready to terrain associate. We begin by plotting our start point and the point we want to travel to on the map. Draw a line that connects the two points, and determine its azimuth, or direction in degrees. We then orient our map and look up at the terrain in front of us along the same azimuth we just plotted. With one or two prominent terrain features as a guide, we can often visualize the route we need to travel to get to our point. The process is much faster and easier than stopping to shoot an azimuth every couple hundred yards.

NIGHT NAVIGATION

This is the hardest form of land navigation because we often can't see more than a foot or two in front of us. Most institutions will teach stu-

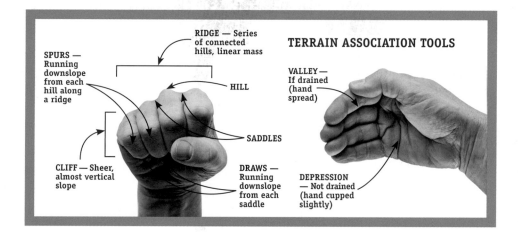

TERRAIN ASSOCIATION TOOLS

SPURS — Running downslope from each hill along a ridge

RIDGE — Series of connected hills, linear mass

HILL

SADDLES

CLIFF — Sheer, almost vertical slope

DRAWS — Running downslope from each saddle

VALLEY — If drained (hand spread)

DEPRESSION — Not drained (hand cupped slightly)

dents to shoot an azimuth as far as they can see, walk to that point, then repeat the process over and over again until they get to where they need to be. This is incredibly slow and makes it hard to keep an accurate pace count to know how far we've traveled.

A trick I figured out in Ranger School was that if I could see the stars on the horizon, I could shoot my azimuth to an easily recognizable star or formation, then just keep walking toward that. I had to be careful to remember which star was mine, but it wasn't too difficult, as I often found either a really bright one or an odd formation of stars that was easy to follow. (Only use stars on the horizon. Using a star overhead is like trying to stay directly under the sun. It won't work.) It is also a good idea to reshoot the azimuth every 15 to 20 minutes because the stars move just like the sun does in the daytime.

Night navigation is also much easier in the winter when there's no vegetation on the trees, allowing more ambient light from the moon and stars to illuminate the ground we're trying to cover. Often we can't control the time of year we're navigating, but if we can, winter navigation is easier than summer.

Another important trick for nighttime navigation is to never lock our knees when we walk. It's a tough habit to break, as we live our entire lives walking like normal people do. We usually lock our knees

New and old-school: Both the GPS and the protractor have their place in land navigation. The protractor should always be our primary navigation technique.

when we extend our leg forward to take a step. Right before our heel strikes the ground, our knee is probably locked. If we do this at night, it's only a matter of time before we hyperextend our knee.

Depth perception is almost impossible at night because it's dark and we can't see well. Even with night vision

goggles, we have terrible depth perception at night. While we expect the ground in front of us to be on the same plane as that on which we're standing, sometimes it isn't. Usually, our eyes give us a heads-up that there's a problem ahead, so we're kind of screwed without them in the dark. This can present a huge problem if we step into a hole or unexpected depression.

Cammenga Compass

TYPE	Lensatic compass
WATERPROOF	Yes
MSRP	$63
MANUFACTURER	Cammenga 313-914-7160 cammenga.com

The Cammenga compass will be most familiar to those who learned to navigate in the military. Suunto also offers an excellent model, the MC-2.

Suunto MC-2

TYPE	Lensatic compass
WATERPROOF	Yes
MSRP	$56
MANUFACTURER	Suunto 800-426-4840 rei.com

Stepping into a hole with a locked knee transfers our entire body weight and all the weight we're carrying directly to our knee after giving our load a running start and some time in free-fall. If we're lucky, we experience pain and then get to walk it off. If we're unlucky, we tear something important and we're officially screwed. The latter happens all the time when people start to hustle through the woods carrying heavy packs at night.

The preventative measure is simple and easy but requires us to pay attention to what we're doing. Do not lock your knees when walking at night. That's all. With a slightly flexed knee, we turn our leg into a shock absorber that can take an unexpected load. If we really want to be cautious, collapse the leg as soon as it hits the ground after an unexpected drop. The knee takes no abuse if we do this because we transfer the shock to our ass or side (if we flop over, which is smart) instead.

CRUCIAL GEAR

The four most important pieces of navigation equipment are a map, a compass, a protractor and a pencil. Nothing too exotic here.

We should laminate map sheets that we use frequently because an unprotected map will quickly become unreadable and disintegrate once exposed to dirt and water. If we choose to navigate with an unprotected map, it is best to

NavELite Trekker H	
TYPE	Wrist compass
WATERPROOF	No (water resistant)
MSRP	$80
MANUFACTURER	NavELite 336-509-9924 navelite.com

The NavELite wrist compass is the best the author has found among available models. The Garmin Tactix is brand new and combines time-telling with a GPS that displays coordinates in both MGRS and lat/long. It also gives the times for sunrise and sunset — valuable information when you're moving for hours at a time.

Garmin Tactix	
TYPE	GPS watch
WATERPROOF	Yes
MSRP	$450
MANUFACTURER	Garmin 312-787-3221 garmin.com

keep it in a waterproof bag. An easy way to make one is to get a Ziploc sandwich bag and cover it with duct tape. They fit into a cargo pocket and will not puncture easily.

The protractor is a small piece of plastic with cut-outs for grid squares of various sizes. We can poke a small hole directly in the center where the "crosshairs" intersect, push a piece of twine (550 gut works well) through the hole and tie a knot at both ends of the twine to keep it from pulling through the hole. The twine allows us to connect points to find our

azimuth without having to draw on our map. Make sure the twine passes directly through the center of the protractor or the azimuths will always be wrong.

I still favor the military-issue lensatic compass. It's made by Cammenga and can be found for right around $65. It has tritium where we need it, and the piece of string trapped in the lid makes shooting azimuths a snap.

Suunto offers a high-quality compass, the MC-2, for a bit less money. It has a mirror on its lid, so our methodology for shooting azimuths changes. The clear body has various measuring units that allow us to easily measure the distance of our routes. It is a quality product that works well.

GUCCI GEAR

There are some pieces of gear that aren't critical for our navigation success, but they sure do make it easier. The most useful of these is a quality wrist compass. A wrist compass doesn't offer the precision of a regular compass, but it does allow us to maintain an "accurate enough" azimuth while we're moving, especially if we have some terrain features to help us out.

The NavELite Trekker H is easily the best example of a wrist compass that I've seen. It has a thick rubber wristband that doesn't absorb sweat, so it will never develop an odor. It is also thick enough that it would be extremely hard to strip the compass off a wrist, even if someone tried to grab it and take it.

A wrist compass is great for fast land navigation, determining cardinal directions for times we choose to orient our map (which should be often) and boxing around obstacles. It saves us from having to dig out our regular compass and stow it each time we need an azimuth check. A wrist compass is a good idea, and the Trekker H is the best I've seen.

Another key piece of Gucci gear is the GPS. A GPS is an ancillary piece of equipment and should never be used for primary navigation because it can lose its signal if we have steep terrain around us or thick overhead cover. Another problem with GPS-only navigation is that it will take you directly to your point and won't account for cliffs, draws, swamps or depressions. Each one of these can provide a miserable experience if we don't avoid them.

The Garmin Rhino is a sweet GPS that also functions as a walkie-talkie. It's a great way to trim two pieces of gear down to one and has some trick features that really benefit the owner when hunting or working in groups. However, if we don't need the combination of walkie-talkie and GPS, there are other GPS units that serve us better.

My favorite GPS is the new Garmin Tactix. It sets itself apart from other similar models because it offers a tremendous amount of relevant features. The Tactix can be used as a magnetic compass while stationary, displays grids in both military grid reference system (MGRS) and lat/long, and gives us sunrise/sunset times for our location. It's also a watch.

TIME IN THE SADDLE

Land navigation gets easier the more we practice it. We should expect to get disoriented (but never lost) while we learn. Also, we'll likely spend some time in a draw learning that we really don't want to be there no matter how much shorter our route would be if we just cut through it. These are valuable lessons that teach us the intricacies of navigation. It just takes some time doing it before those lessons really settle in.

As a hunter, search-and-rescue person, or military member, we'll all need to navigate through the woods at some point. The most important aspect of learning to navigate is to get out and do it. The tips covered here will spare you some pain and make the learning process a bit faster.

MISFIRES

THE TRUTH ABOUT PRIMER RELIABILITY AND SENSITIVITY.

BY JEFF HOFFMAN

L et's say you were just out training and experienced a misfire. You replaced the round in the chamber and hit it again. The damned thing still didn't go off! The primer hit is deep, and to top it off, later in the day you have another misfire. Bad ammo, right? Maybe not.

PRIMER RELIABILITY

Primers are constructed of three basic components: a cup, which is the part that is visible at the base of a cartridge case; an anvil, which is a small, tripod-shaped piece of metal; and an impact-sensitive explosive, normally lead styphnate. Just like the name suggests, the cup is shaped like a cup and contains the explosive primer mix sandwiched between the bottom of the cup and the anvil. Primers are designed to be struck in the center by the firing pin with a specified force in order to ignite the cartridge. When the primer is struck, the cup indents

inward, causing a shearing action on the impact-sensitive explosive as the firing pin crushes it against the anvil in the primer, detonating the primer. Primers ignite with incredible reliability. In the words of notable Winchester ballistician Glen Weeks:

"Based on the SAAMI-specified drop test, statistics will tell you that our primers are 99.9997 percent reliable. That means that when struck with sufficient energy and properly centered, they will go off 99.9997 percent of the time. A lead-styphnate primer is probably one of the oldest and most reliable devices on the planet."

Misfires do happen, but misfires due to a defective primer are very rare. My company, Black Hills Ammunition, test fires more than 100,000 rounds per year, every year. It sells tens of millions of rounds each year to customers who are very demanding. When a misfire is encountered during testing, or if a misfire is reported by a customer, the company fully investigates the cause. These investigations over the years have shown that misfires were the result of a defective primer in only a very small percentage of the incidents.

The point is about statistics. Primers are not perfect—nothing man-made is—but they are very

reliable. Statistically, you might encounter a defective primer, if you shoot enough. Mr. Weeks's data indicates 99.9997 percent reliability. That means you might hit a misfire every 300,000 rounds. Black Hills' experience does not indicate even that high of a misfire rate. The company visually inspects every one of the many millions of primers it gets yearly from Winchester and other primer manufacturers before they go to the loading operation. Over the years, the average is one rejected primer in about every 250,000, but most of the flaws are minor defects or damage such as slightly out-of-round primers that would have no effect on reliability. The company can't visually inspect the interior of primers that come to it in the form of primed brass such as the .308 brass, but it does inspect for proper insertion, appearance and depth.

In the scenario we started with, our hypothetical shooter had two misfires in one training session. The odds of encountering two misfires due to defective primers in one day are beyond remote. "So," you ask, "what can cause this type of misfire situation if it isn't defective primers in most of the cases?" There are a number of possibilities.

DENTS IN PRIMERS

The most common general cause of misfires is what's termed "insufficient indent." That means the primer was not struck with sufficient force. You say, "Look at the indent. It was huge. I even hit it several times, and it still didn't go." Primers are set up with a very precise orientation of primer component parts. If the primer is hit once and it does not go off due to insufficient firing-pin force, the sensitivity is further decreased. The primer mix, called a pellet, may have been cracked and moved out of the way from between the cup and the anvil. The primer mix is intended to detonate when sheared between the cup and the anvil by the primer strike. If the first blow is insufficient, the second one is now trying to ignite a primer that was damaged by the first strike. Sometimes the primer will go with a follow-up hit, and sometimes it won't.

Hitting it again doesn't prove anything either way. It does, however, make the indent deeper so it looks to the average viewer that it certainly should have gone off. It also destroys the evidence necessary to do a good investigation. Therefore, if you have a misfire and want to investigate the cause, do not try firing the round again. Think of it as similar to a car accident investigation. Would it be good scene preservation to have the cars back up and hit each other again to help you analyze the physical evidence? If you want to know why a primer

The cartridge on the left shows clear indications of insufficient firing-pin indent. The right primer has been properly struck.

did not go off, save the misfired round along with the box it came in and contact the manufacturer for instructions on returning it for examination.

FIREARM-INDUCED MISFIRES

How can a firearm cause a misfire due to an insufficient indent? One possibility is a damaged firing pin, one that has either a bent or chipped tip. Another possibility is that the firing-pin spring is too weak. The spring may be dragging on the interior of the bolt body or impeded by grease in the bolt, especially under cold conditions. The pin may be dragging on an improperly aligned firing-pin aperture, or it may be too short. Misfires can even be caused by excessive headspace. Basically, headspace is the measurement from the slope of the shoulder to the base of the cartridge, or the corresponding dimensions in the rifle chamber. Excessive chamber headspace allows the cartridge

to be farther forward in the chamber away from the firing pin, or it can allow for the cartridge case to move forward when struck by the firing pin. Certainly, this can affect ignition reliability and cause misfires.

IMPROPER LOADING TECHNIQUES

Improper loading techniques can cause perfectly good primers to perform poorly. For best sensitivity, the primer should be seated firmly to the bottom of the primer pocket, but not unduly crushed into place. The legs of the anvil are slightly compressed during the seating process, which can cock or tilt the primer. If the primer is not seated to the bottom of the primer pocket, it's not as sensitive, and the primer can also move forward slightly upon impact by the firing pin, cushioning the impact force. Conversely, if the primer is seated with too much force, it sits deep in the primer pocket, causing it to be farther from the normal position for firing-pin impact, and the primer anvil can be pushed through the primer mix to the bottom of the primer cup. If there is insufficient mix remaining between the cup and anvil, the result is a misfire.

If a cartridge case has insufficient headspace due to a manufacturing defect, misfires can result. If the case is undersize, it can move forward in the chamber upon firing-pin impact just as if the chamber were too long. Contamination of the primer by moisture or oil can also desensitize the primer, resulting in a misfire. These causes are not typically seen in factory-loaded ammunition due to quality-control procedures. They are more commonly seen with handloaded ammunition.

SHOOTER-INDUCED MISFIRES

Another common cause for misfires from a perfectly functioning rifle and good ammunition is failure of the operator to completely close the bolt before firing. If the bolt handle is lifted even slightly from the completely

Primers are incredibly reliable when properly struck with industry-specified firing-pin impact force.

closed position, a misfire can result. I discussed this with George Gardner of GA Precision. He advises:

"It's very common for the user to get caught up in the moment of a match or training exercise and blow one of the easiest things to do—close the bolt completely. Speed is not always the best option, as smooth is faster. When the bolt is not fully closed, the firing-pin cocking piece drops onto the camming surface of the bolt and not in the open notch that is there for clearance. This robs a lot of the energy from the firing pin."

I suggest you try this demonstration the next time you go to the range. Unload your rifle. Double-check to make sure it is unloaded. Close the bolt, then raise the bolt very slightly. Squeeze the trigger while watching the bolt

handle. You can see the bolt handle snap closed. The energy to make that happen is being robbed from the firing-pin velocity and energy normally used to strike the primer. Failure to completely close the bolt is easy to do, especially under speed drills, stress and position shooting. Normally, we get away with it. Sometimes it induces a misfire. I discussed this with Charlie Milazzo, firearms advisor to the American Sniper Association (ASA). He said, "Failure to completely close the bolt is probably the single most common cause of all misfires in sniper rifles."

DIFFERENCES IN BRANDS

As an ammunition manufacturer at Black Hills Ammunition, I have the obligation and opportunity to investigate misfires. One common situation is that the shooter reports, "I know it can't be anything wrong with my rifle because I've never had a misfire with brand XYZ." While all U.S. primers are made to an industry specification, the specification is a range, not a specific, absolute, identical performance standard. Some brands of primers are more sensitive than others. This isn't because of quality differences, it's by design.

Everything in life is a compromise. Primer manufacturers have to make choices. My company, Black Hills Ammunition, uses Winchester primers. I have discussed this topic at length with Winchester. The company could make its primers more sensitive, but that increases the possibility of a slam-fire. A slam-fire is the premature detonation of the round in the firearm from impact by the bolt or, in some cases, an inadequately restrained firing pin. This can happen most frequently during the feeding process and prior to the round being fully chambered in a semiautomatic or automatic firearm. Consequences of a slam-fire are generally more serious than a misfire from a light strike (60,000 psi of escaping gases from the breech area and next to your face is not a good thing). Military primers are made with an even thicker cup than the one used in commercial primers—specifically for this reason. Think about that. If a sniper rifle will work only with its favorite brand of commercial ammunition, what would happen if you fed it MIL-SPEC ammunition?

Winchester advises that it could also make primers more sensitive by using a different anvil configuration, but while this increases sensitivity to centered primer hits, it decreases sensitivity to slightly off-center hits. Winchester chose to stay with safe, reliable performance in a wide range of circumstances. Primer manufacturers and ammunition manufacturers have to load for everyone's rifle. Most snipers shoot bolt-action rifles. However, ammunition manufacturers have to make ammunition that is safe in every rifle out there. They can't make primers more sensitive and label them "Not for use in semi-automatic rifles." Do not confuse sensitivity with reliability. Primers are incredibly reliable when struck with industry-specified force.

So what does it mean when the rifle experiences no misfires with one brand of ammunition and primer but has misfires with other brands? My opinion (and that of Charlie Milazzo) is that such a rifle is marginal in performance. The sniper using such a rifle is betting against fate that the rifle will work when he needs it. I suggest he resolve the light-strike issue with the rifle, then use whatever brand of primer and ammunition he prefers.

DAMAGED BY CONDITIONS

Ammunition can become contaminated. The most common culprit is light penetrating oil. Oil is an extremely effective desensitizer of primers. That's the biggest reason why most ammunition has lacquer-sealed primers. Moisture can also damage primers, but moisture is not nearly as likely as light penetrating oil to actually penetrate into the primer. Brief exposure to moisture in the field is normally well tolerated by ammunition. Long-term exposure such as storage in damp conditions can destroy ammunition (and so can pressurized water exposure such as diving with your ammunition).

BLAME

Misfires are not that uncommon. Misfires due to a defective primer, however, are rare. That means that if you have a misfire, you should thoroughly have it investigated to determine the cause so you can fix the problem. You don't want a misfire during a critical incident. Don't just chalk up the next one as a bad round and move on. Any sniper, team leader or commander who accepts misfires and does nothing to investigate and fix the problem is making a mistake that can have severe consequences. As professionals, when we identify a problem, we are obligated to determine the cause and take preventative action.

The most common cause of misfires in a bolt-action rifle is operator error. This is often masked, because the bolt closes completely upon pulling the trigger. The good news is that this problem can be corrected though awareness, training and diligence on the part of the operator. If you're confident that the misfire was not due to operator error, save the round and the box it came in, and contact the ammunition manufacturer so that it can investigate. A reputable manufacturer will cooperate fully with your request to have the ammunition examined to determine the cause of the misfire. Do not try to fire the round a second time, because that hampers the ability of the ammunition manufacturer to investigate the misfire. You should also have the rifle thoroughly checked by its manufacturer. When you call, be sure to let the manufacturer know that yours is a sniper's rifle. This should aid in getting a thorough and prompt response from the company.

As a sniper, you train hard to make sure you are capable of doing your job when called upon. It is not unreasonable to expect the same level of reliable performance from your rifle and ammunition.

Jeff Hoffman has been a law enforcement sniper since 1989. He is a reserve deputy in Pennington County, South Dakota, and a sniper team leader of the Pennington County/Rapid City SRT. He is president and co-owner of Black Hills Ammunition Inc.

PRACTICAL

BALLISTICS

CLOSING THE GAP BETWEEN SCIENCE AND APPLICATION.

BY Bryan Litz

External ballistics is the science of bullet flight and is part of the diverse skill set required to hit targets at long range. When science is applied in the real world, especially in a field environment, compromises are a necessary evil; perfect data just isn't available. How much the compromise affects your ability to hit targets will depend on your tools—and more important—your knowledge of how to use them properly. This chapter will explore the application of external ballistics to tactical-shooting scenarios, focusing on how to close the gap between pure science and practical application.

TOOLS OF THE TRADE

There are three primary classes of tools that you'll use when applying ballistics in the field:

1. TOOLS FOR RAW DATA COLLECTION. These are things such as rangefinders (LRFs, maps, ranging reticles), Kestrel or other weather measuring tools, angle cosine indicators, etc. Basically, they're the measurement tools you need to gather the information required to support a scientific calculation. The more refined and accurate your measurements are, the more accurate your ballistic solutions will be.

2. THE BALLISTIC SOLVER. The purpose of this tool is to bridge the gap between raw data and useful fire solutions. These come in many forms, including PDAs, smartphones, nomograms (like the Accuracy 1st Whiz Wheel) and basic range cards. It's important to note that some solvers are inherently more accurate than others, but no solver is more accurate than the raw data supplied to it.

3. THE RIFLESCOPE. In terms of ballistics, the purpose of the scope is to enable the shooter to apply the calculated fire solution via dials or reticle with as little error as possible. This is a demanding task that's often taken for granted.

You can think of these three classes of tools as links in a chain. Raw data supports a calculation, and the riflescope applies that calculation. As with any chain, it's no stronger than its weakest link. In a perfect world, raw data

measurements would be complete and perfect every time. That perfect data would drive a perfect ballistic calculation, and the scope would allow the shooter to apply the fire

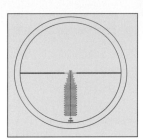
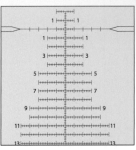

A good reticle like the Horus enables the shooter to accurately apply his ballistic solution. This modern reticle is a better application tool for the firing solution than using the dials of the scope.

solution with no error. Obviously, we don't live in a perfect world. What we can do is learn how to do the most with what we have and close the gap as much as possible.

Great amounts could be (and have been) written on each of the three classes of tools. From how to refine your use of a ranging reticle to verifying that your scope dials are producing the desired corrections, it's a lot of information. The remainder of this chapter will focus on the ballistic solver.

Essentially, the ballistic solver is applying the equations of projectile motion to simulate a ballistic

trajectory. This requires accurate models of the target, atmosphere, projectile and the initial conditions. Of the variables required to predict bullet drop, there are only a couple that are difficult to nail down with certainty: the muzzle velocity (MV) and ballistic coefficient (BC).

Muzzle velocity is difficult to know because you need a chronograph to measure it directly. Even then, most chronographs are not as accurate as they're thought to be. Furthermore, access to chronographs for military snipers is not always assured. Due to these challenges, it's common to have a degree of uncertainty related to muzzle velocity. You can make an intelligent assumption about your muzzle velocity by shooting at a distant target, observing your drop and adjusting the velocity input to your ballistic solver until the prediction matches the observed drop. Some programs even have built-in functions that automatically find the MV based on observed

The angle-degree indicator from Nightforce shows the degree of bore slope and mounts to a Picatinny rail. The Kestrel combines both abilities to collect atmospheric data with an exceptional ballistic solver program.

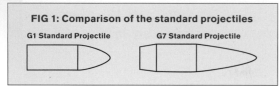

FIG 1: Comparison of the standard projectiles

G1 Standard Projectile   G7 Standard Projectile

drop. Caution is advised when conducting this exercise, though, as any error or uncertainty in the observation will bias the calibration and your future predictions will be off as a result. Best practice is to shoot to the supersonic extent of your weapon system to determine MV, as this will minimize (but not eliminate) experimental error (more on this later).

Having an accurate BC is even more challenging, and as we'll see shortly, even the most accurate BC may not be an adequate model at transonic speed.

A bullet's BC is a measure of how well a bullet retains velocity. There's lots of smoke and mirrors surrounding the actual meaning of the BC, but it's actually quite simple to understand. Mathematically, the BC is the sectional density (SD) divided by a form factor. SD is a familiar term and is easy to calculate:

SD = bullet weight/7,000/ caliber squared. For example, a 175-grain .308 bullet has an SD of 175/7,000/.308² = .264.

BC is simply the SD divided by a form factor. Form factor is just a comparison of a particular bullet's drag

to the drag of a standard projectile. There are many standard projectiles; G1 and G7 are the ones in most common use. Suppose you compared the drag of a bullet with the G1 standard and found your bullet had 55.6 percent the drag of that standard projectile. That means your bullet has a G1 form factor of .556. If we're talking about the .30-caliber 175-grain SMK, which has an SD of .264, that bullet would have a G1 BC of .264/.556 = .475. In fact, this is the measured form factor and BC for that bullet between 3,000 and 1,500 feet per second.

The G7 BC is the same math, only referring to the G7 curve instead of G1. The G7 form factor of the 175 SMK is 1.086, so the G7 BC is .264/1.086 = .243.

The form factors are so different because the G1 and G7 projectiles and drag curves are dramatically different (see Figures 1 and 2).

The Vecronix **SORD** combines the laser range-finder with the Horus ballistic solver program. When used together the two generate a near-instantaneous firing solution.

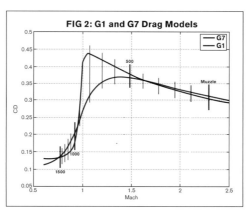

FIG 2: G1 and G7 Drag Models

Range (m)	175 SMK @ 2,550 fps Sea Level Conditions		
	G1 BC .475	G7 BC .243	Different
	Trajectory (MILS)		
100	0	0	0
200	-0.61	-.61	0
300	-1.57	-1.56	.01
400	-2.73	-2.72	.01
500	-4.08	-4.05	.03
600	-5.64	-5.6	.04
700	-7.43	-7.38	.05
800	-9.49	-9.46	.03
900	-11.86	-11.9	-.04
1,000	-14.56	-14.74	-.18
1,100	-17.6	-17.99	-.39
1,200	-20.99	-21.62	-.63
1,300	-24.74	-25.6	-.86
1,400	-28.83	-29.93	-1.1
1,500	-33.26	-34.6	-1.34

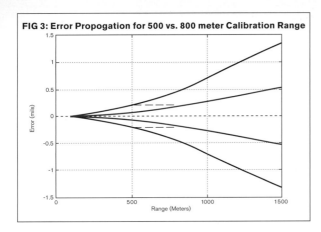

FIG 3: Error Propogation for 500 vs. 800 meter Calibration Range

| | Actual MV | .2 MIL Calibration Error At: | | | |
| | | 800 meters | | 500 meters | |
Range (m)	2,550	2,570	Error	2,600	Error
100	.00	.00	.00	.00	.00
200	-.61	-.59	.02	-.57	.04
300	-1.56	-1.53	.03	-1.48	.08
400	-2.71	-2.66	.05	-2.58	.13
500	-4.05	-3.97	.08	-3.86	.19
600	-5.59	-5.48	.11	-5.33	.26
700	-7.37	-7.23	.14	-7.02	.35
800	-9.44	-9.26	.19	-9.00	.44
900	-11.88	-11.65	.23	-11.31	.57
1000	-14.72	-14.43	.29	-14.02	.70
1,100	-17.96	-17.63	.33	-17.13	.83
1,200	-21.59	-21.20	.39	-20.62	.97
1,300	-25.56	-25.12	.44	-24.47	1.09
1,400	-29.89	-29.40	.49	-28.67	1.22
1,500	-34.55	-34.01	.54	-33.21	1.34

The drag curves depicted in Figure 2 are representing the drag coefficient as a function of Mach number. There's a lot of science behind this plot that we don't need to get into. For our purposes, simply note that these models are scaled to represent drag in a ballistics program, when using G1 or G7 BCs. How well your bullet matches the drag model will affect how accurately the ballistic solver can predict that bullet's trajectory.

Notice that at supersonic speeds, the G1 and G7 drag curves are very similar in shape. That means that if an accurate form factor is used, both the G1 and G7 BCs can model very accurate trajectories for bullets in their supersonic range of flight.

However, look at how the drag curves compare in the transonic range of flight. The G7 drag model has proportionally more drag at transonic speed compared with the G1 drag curve, and by a significant margin. In fact, transonic speed is where drag models diverge the most. As a result of the divergence in drag models at transonic speed, ballistic solvers can calculate different transonic trajectories for G1 versus G7 BC models.

There are several interesting things to see in Figure 2. Note how smooth and parallel the G1 and G7 curves are from the muzzle

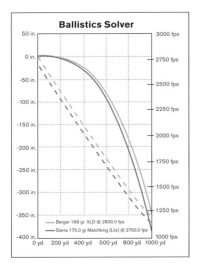

Ballistics Solver

— Berger 168 gr. VLD @ 2800.0 fps
— Sierra 175.0 gr Matchking (Litz) @ 2700.0 fps

to about 500 meters. Over this range, the G1 versus G7 predicted trajectories are very similar, within .1 mil. From the muzzle to 400 meters, the G1 BC is modeling drag a little bit higher than the G7 BC. As a result, the G1 BC is predicting slightly more drop, but not much. Due to the higher drag modeled early in the G1 trajectory, the bullet is predicted to have more drop, even hundreds of yards beyond where the curves cross. In other words, since G1 modeled more drag early in the flight, and less drag later, the cumulative drop is not very different compared with the G7-based prediction from zero to about 800 meters. After 800 meters, the higher transonic drag of the G7 model results in much more drop than the G1 trajectory.

So what's this mean in terms of practical application? For one, it means that you could true your ballistic solver for MV at 800 meters and see essentially zero error in trajectory prediction due to the different drag curves from the muzzle to transonic. But after transonic (800 meters in this case), the divergence of the drag curves results in increasing separation between the G1- and G7-based trajectories.

In reality, the .30-cal. 175-grain SMK has a unique drag curve that doesn't perfectly match either the G1 or the G7 curve. In fact, the custom drag model for the 175 SMK is about halfway between the G1 and G7 model. As a result, the actual drop of that bullet would be about halfway between that predicted by G1 and G7 tables above.

When shooting into the transonic range of your bullet's trajectory, you have to account for the transonic effects on drag. The most common-sense way is to true BC in a similar way that MV is trued over supersonic range. Procedures for truing BC in trans/subsonic vary by application, and we won't get into that here. Basically, you're observing the bullet's actual drop and using that information to modify the drag curve for future calculations. The closer the drag model (G1 or G7) matches your bullet,

the less truing, or correction, will be required. Of course, the best approach is to start off by modeling the actual custom drag curve for your bullet if your software allows. Truing may still be required, but there will be much less error to true if you start with a more accurate drag model.

In both the supersonic and transonic portions of the trajectory, it's important to extend the distance between truing points as much as possible to minimize experimental error. Figure 3 demonstrates this concept visually.

SUMMARY

This chapter began by putting ballistic predictions into context as one of the many tasks a long-range shooter has to master for success. Even when isolated, trajectory prediction is still a vast subject area, and we've only focused on one very narrow portion of it: error management.

To review, the modern (properly written) ballistic solver can predict trajectories as accurate as the data supplied to it. Given perfect data, ballistic solvers can predict equally accurate trajectories. Any imperfections in predictions stem from inaccuracies in describing your projectile, environment or target. The field environment is far from the perfect-world scenario, so many of the ballistic inputs are estimates and intelligent assumptions, which compromise the accuracy of trajectory predictions.

The well-educated sniper knows how to manage these uncertainties with field-expedient methods that bring the predictions closer to reality.

Muzzle velocity is a fundamentally important variable that you probably won't know with perfect accuracy. One field-expedient approach to correcting this variable is to shoot to the supersonic limit of the trajectory, observe the bullet drop and use it to correct the MV input. Over the supersonic range of the bullet, MV is the biggest uncertainty, and differences in drag modeling (G1 versus G7) are minor. It's important that you choose a range at the supersonic extent of the trajectory to minimize experimental error.

When the bullet slows to transonic speed, the drag modeling can become an issue. This can be field-corrected (trued) in much the same way as the MV input. For best results, care must be taken to choose the truing ranges in terms of the transonic zone. Any error that's incurred in the process of truing the ballistic solver will become a permanent, built-in bias to all future calculations. Remember, truing is a calibration exercise and, as such, must be done with extreme discretion.

REFERENCES

Bryan Litz: "Applied Ballistics for Long Range Shooting," Second Edition, Applied Ballistics, LLC, Cedar Springs, MI, 2011

Bryan Litz: "Accuracy and Precision for Long Range Shooting," Applied Ballistics, LLC, Cedar Springs, MI, 2012

PART II
GUNS AND GEAR

THE SNIPER'S ULTIMATE "ONE GUN"

THE WINDS OF CHANGE ARE BLOWING IN SNIPERLAND. HERE'S WHAT'S COMING.

BY TOM BECKSTRAND // PHOTOS BY MARK FINGAR

The role of the sniper and what constitutes a sniper rifle are hotly debated topics. Many firearm enthusiasts define a sniper as a "one shot, one kill" perfectionist who must infiltrate the target area unnoticed, hit the target and then vanish into thin air. That certainly qualifies as a sniper, but we should not limit ourselves doctrinally by clinging to the belief that that is the *only* definition of a sniper.

Chambered in 7.62x51mm, the LaRue OBR features an integral triggerguard and beveled magazine well. The triggerguard doesn't create a blister on the firing hand's middle finger, and the mag well facilitates smooth reloads.

One of the most well-known snipers from World War II was Vasily Zaytsev. Zaytsev made a name for himself during the Battle of Stalingrad, where he crawled around the destroyed city for just over a month in late 1942 killing more than 200 German soldiers—and did it all with a bolt-action Mosin-Nagant.

Another well-known figure prominent in any sniper's landscape is Carlos Hathcock. The Gunnery Sergeant executed feats of

Photos by Mark Fingar

Two Special Forces snipers engage targets at the USASOC sniper competition held at Fort Bragg. This picture illustrates a typical arrangement where one sniper carries a bolt rifle for the really long engagements and the other utilizes a semiauto for targets 800 yards and in.

A team equipped with a LaRue OBR and MK 13 work their way through the daytime stress event. The USASOC sniper competition lasts a week and covers both rural and urban sniping.

Photos by Mark Fingar

A fast-roping sniper hits a snag as the long barrel of his rifle catches a wind sill on the structure. This is just one of those times where a long barrel is not a sniper's friend.

almost incomprehensible skill. He crawled for four days and three nights to kill a Vietnamese general. He shot an enemy sniper through the tube of his scope moments before the enemy sniper would have killed him. Like Zaytsev, Gunnery Sergeant Hathcock did all of this with a bolt-action rifle.

From these two impressive historical figures, many draw their doctrinal definition of what a sniper does, how he does it and what equipment he uses. While this methodology of sniping is still relevant today, the deliberate stalks, calculated movement and single killing shots represent only half of

what today's sniper must face.

Today's sniper must also perform on a more nebulous battlefield populated with urbanized insurgents. Insurgents are impossible to distinguish visually from innocent civilians, so a sniper often doesn't know what his target is until it's shooting at him. Gunfights are almost always fast and chaotic, so today's sniper must equip himself in a manner that enables him to appropriately deal with this type of threat.

URBAN VERSUS RURAL
If you've ever attended any one of the U.S. Army's or Marine Corps' sniper schools,

you've spent a considerable amount of time crawling on your belly. This is classic sniper tradecraft employed in rural environments. This

The rounded OBR handguard lends itself well to position shooting. The removable Picatinny rail sections allow placement of components only where they are needed.

Although LaRue has many stock options, this Magpul PRS stock is highly regarded on scoped applications for its adjustable cheekrest and adjustable length of pull.

Photos by Mark Fingar

SFC Giannelli, one of two winners in this year's International Sniper Competition, poses with the OBR he used in competition. His OBR features a 16-inch barrel, Magpul PRS stock and US Optics SN3 scope.

is where we find our drag-bags, ghillie suits, pruning shears, face paint and a number of other very manly accoutrements.

Sniping in a rural environment is why militaries of the world still cling to the bolt-action rifle as their primary sniping firearm. This is the only environment in which such a weapon system makes sense. If not kept in check, militaries will develop their sniping rifles solely around this sniping role and our bolt-action rifles get heavier and heavier.

If you look at the bolt-action sniping rifles from Vietnam (where we did some serious shooting), you'll notice that they bear much more resemblance to a hunting rifle than to the monstrous M40A3 that the Marine Corps hoists onto today's Devil Dog. Some would argue that the M40 has evolved. Evolution shouldn't mean that you now have to hump around a rifle that's twice as heavy as the original, sports a monstrous prone stock that seriously inhibits positional shooting and still doesn't offer you any more compatibility with night vision equipment or infrared lasers than the rifle your dad toted around Vietnam. Is that evolution?

When we enter the world of military sniping in an urban environment, the bolt-action rifle becomes a huge liability and the short-barreled semiautomatic sniper rifle really shines. Sniping is much more than lying behind the rifle and pulling the trigger, especially in urbanized terrain. Snipers cannot miracle themselves into their firing points and must be able to move securely from their infiltration platform to the firing point, a repetitive process that can occur several times over several days and often requires some running and gunning along the way.

A sniper team on the move in an urban setting still consists of a sniper and a spotter. The problem created when the sniper carries a bolt-action rifle is that he cannot effectively clear corners, stairwells or rooms and so places his M4-armed spotter in greater danger. Remember, at a minimum it takes two appropriately equipped men to enter and clear a room, and a bolt-action rifle isn't appropriate for this task. If the sniper

were carrying, say, a 16-inch-barreled semiautomatic 7.62mm, he could effectively do everything his spotter could do with the M4 and still be exceptionally well equipped for any sniping task placed before him.

IS 16 INCHES ENOUGH?

I can hear the cries of "Blasphemy!" already. Surely, no serious sniper would ever be caught dead with a 16-inch barrel on his rifle. Some would falsely argue that the shorter barrel would be less accurate. That is absolutely incorrect. The only disadvantage associated with a shorter barrel is a loss in muzzle velocity.

The downside of a lower muzzle velocity is that it can create weaker terminal ballistics and has a more parabolic flight path for the projectile. If we were talking about the 5.56mm round, I'd

lend some serious credence to the short barrel/weaker terminal ballistics argument. However, given the 168- to 175-grain mass of the 7.62mm projectile, I think that even 1,000 fps would prove to be lethal. Even with a 16-inch barrel, the military load for 7.62mm will still retain 1,000 fps out to 800 to 900 yards.

The increasingly parabolic flight of the round that comes with lower muzzle velocities used to mean that the sniper would have to spend more time building an accurate data book. There would have been more

This SF sniper is competing in the USASOC sniper competition with a suppressed LaRue OBR and a US Optics SN3 scope with Horus reticle.

elevation variation as the distance to the target changed, requiring more data points for an accurate book. However, with the advent of the Horus reticle, handheld ballistic computers and now the Whiz Wheel, there is no longer the need for a sniper to build a data book. These tools enable the sniper to true his rifle to computer algorithms and know within 1/100 of a mil where to hold to hit the target. Yes, this is really possible.

Fact is, semiautomatic is better than bolt-action when militaries are sniping with the 7.62x51mm cartridge. The 7.62 NATO, in military dress, pushes a 175-grain bullet at about 2,675 fps out of the M24 and M40A3. Shorten the barrel to 16 inches like the LaRue OBR does and the velocity drops to around 2,550 fps. This is not a substantial loss. What the LaRue OBR allows that a bolt-action rifle doesn't is that the sniper can effectively fight like a rifleman until he needs to start sniping. Entering and clearing buildings, running up stairwells and engaging multiple targets are now well within his capabilities. Good luck doing all of that with a bolt action.

Please don't think I'm a bolt-action hater. I have a gang of bolt-action rifles, and I love them all. Bolt-action rifles are great because they're simple to manipulate, can digest a wider range of bullet weights and velocities, and offer the shooter more control of when the round enters the chamber. They are an excellent choice for law enforcement sniping. While I loathe a 16-plus-pound bolt-action 7.62mm sniper rifle, I think a 16-pound (or lighter) bolt-action .338 Lapua Magnum makes wonderful sense for a sniper rifle. Or, if you build a nine- to 10-pound 20-inch-barreled .308 Win. as a sniper rifle and put a hunting stock on it, I think that's OK, too.

INTERNATIONAL SNIPER AND USASOC COMPETITIONS

While it's all well and good for us gun hacks to sit around pontificating about the future of sniping, perhaps some empirical evidence is in order. It just so happens that the U.S. Army hosts a sniping competition that lasts several days and involves competitors from all branches of service, the law enforcement community and even allied countries. Competitors are allowed to enter in two categories, Service Class and Open Class. The Service Class is for teams where both members fire rifles chambered in 7.62x51mm. The Open Class is for competitors firing anything they want.

The 2010 International Sniper Competition and the winning rifles provide us with some insight into what today's most talented snipers carry and shoot when they have a choice. The winners of the Service Class were SFC Chance Giannelli and SFC Ed Hoymeyer. Both men won with the LaRue OBR. Chance's gun had a 16-inch barrel, and Ed's had a 20-inch barrel. A USASOC headquarters team won the Open Class, and the spotter of that team also carried a LaRue OBR. Three out of the four winning rifles were LaRue OBRs. This is what we sometimes refer to as a "clue." It seems the semiauto sniper rifle has quite a following.

Around the time I was writing this chapter, the Army's Special Operations Command hosted its own sniper match at Fort Bragg run by the good men of the Special Forces Sniper School. I hot-footed it down to Bragg to catch up with some old friends and teammates and look in on the match. While I was there I also had the opportunity to interview SFCs Giannelli and Hoymeyer.

One of the first questions I asked both men was why they chose to compete in the International match with the OBR. Chance responded, "My OBR consistently shoots half

MOA. It's fast to get back on target, and recoil management is a nonissue."

Ed said, "My 20-inch OBR shoots 2½-inch groups at 500 yards. It's light, offers fast follow-up shots and doesn't require me to break position shot to shot. It's easy to use for positional shooting."

When I asked Chance if he ever felt outgunned, he said, "The .338 Norma [used by the USASOC headquarters team] was a little intimidating. However, we felt our most serious competitors were Chris and Kevin [fellow Special Forces Sniper Instructors], but they were shooting a different class."

Ed's response bordered on cocky. "No. Even with the Open Class guys."

Knowing that some will pooh-pooh a semiauto sniper rifle because they claim it's not reliable, I asked both Chance and Ed if they'd ever seen or experienced a malfunction with their OBRs. Both men responded "No." Considering the amount of ammunition they've seen put through the platform, I think we can confidently say that a semiauto like the OBR is completely and totally reliable.

The USASOC Sniper Competition provided more evidence of what we saw at the International Sniper Competition. Once again, both members of the winning team were carrying semiauto 7.62mm guns. The match required stalking, shooting unknown distance, movers and a final running and gunning stress event.

THE CHOICE IS CLEAR

Semiauto sniper rifles such as the LaRue OBR are the choice of today's discriminating professional. Men who go into harm's way like the gun because of its accuracy, utter reliability and flexibility of the platform. Integrating the latest lasers, thermals and night vision equipment is a breeze, the rifle lends itself well to positional shooting, and the semiauto action greatly facilitates recoil management. From a sniper's perspective, this is a "do anything" rifle.

While I still see a place on the battlefield for bolt-action rifles, they are more relevant when chambered in cartridges such as the .300 Win. Mag. or .338 Lapua Mag. and employed at ranges beyond 800 meters. For everything closer than 800 in either urban or rural settings, the choice is clear. If you're serious about sniping, shoot the OBR.

PARAGON

WHY THIS .300 WIN. MAG. FROM
AMERICAN PRECISION ARMS
BEATS YOUR .338 LAPUA.

BY Tom Beckstrand

T's hard not to love the .338 Lapua Magnum. With a ballistic coefficient (BC) of .767 in Lapua's 300-grain Scenar load and a muzzle velocity of 2,750 feet per second (fps), it's every long-range shooter's dream. That is until we realize that we have a rifle chambered for $5 bills and one that'll eventually beat the hell out of you after 50 rounds.

The .338 Lapua is an awesome cartridge, and it generates superb external ballistics. However, the rifle platform is often costly, they're very expensive to feed, and the recoil and muzzle blast are spectacular. I think everybody needs to own a .338 Lapua Magnum at some point in life, but before purchasing the Big Dog, I recommend looking at today's .300 Winchester Magnum.

The .300 Win. Mag. languished for many years as a marginal selection for the long-range enthusiast. This was no fault of the caliber itself, but stemmed from the fact that the best bullets available lacked the BCs needed to make the round viable. Sierra had the best offerings, and they only had BCs of .523 for their 190-grain MatchKing (available loaded in Federal Gold Medal Match) and a .607 BC for their 220-grain MatchKing, which I've never seen loaded for sale in any round. We often hear that the best bullets and loads in 6.5mm/.260 will match anything the .300 Win. Mag. can come up with in external ballistics without the recoil, expense and blast. Provided that we stick to the anemic 190-grain MatchKing, this statement is true. Once we look at today's bullets for the .300 Win. Mag., the 6.5mm/.260 argument becomes laughable.

The heart of the Paragon is APA's Genesis action. This action has a one-piece bolt, a superb extractor and a repositioned ejector. It represents an evolution in rifle actions.

Today, there are much better bullets available for the .300 Win. Mag. I spent a large part of one year playing with Hornady's 208-grain A-MAX, which is an amazing bullet and one that I will use for years to come. The 208 A-MAX has a BC of .633, so it beats Sierra's best offering and is also lighter so we can push it at higher velocities. The secant ogive of the 208 A-MAX gives the bullet a great BC, but it will require some manipulation of the seating depth to get it to shoot accurately. That's the problem with secant ogives. They have great BCs, but are finicky. For the 208 A-MAX, the effort is worth the performance.

Another bullet that shows great promise is Berger's new 230-grain hybrid. The hybrid line tries to use properties of both the secant and tangent ogives to provide a high-BC (thanks to the secant shape) while being more forgiving with the seating depth (thanks to the tangent, or more rounded, ogive). Berger's target bullet has a BC of .743, and the tactical bullet has a BC of .714. Now we're in territory that previously was limited to only the big .338. Suddenly, the .300 Win. Mag. just got much more attractive.

AMERICAN PRECISION ARMS

To help me spearhead a .300 Win. Mag. project, I consulted with Jered Joplin, owner of American Precision Arms. I first met Jered years ago when I was still in the Army. I was serving as a sniper team leader and thought it would be a good idea to get a custom rifle built as a "getting out of the Army" present for myself. I asked teammates and instructors who they knew who built a good product, and their responses kept pointing to Jered.

My first rifle-building experience with Jered was painless and the product was superb, so I've been a repeat customer for years. During this time I've learned to give Jered some general guidelines, then let him do his thing. His solutions are always better than mine.

My guidance for Jered on the .300 Win. Mag. project was that I wanted a rifle capable of extreme long-range shooting, yet still portable. I see a lot of monster rifles built that ride the bags or sit well on the bench, but God help the man shooting it if he needs to carry it very far. I wanted as light a contour of barrel as possible without a substantial degradation of accuracy, a muzzlebrake, an action that could double as a family heirloom, detachable box magazines and, if possible, a side-folding stock. Jered and I argued a little on the barrel length and contour, but the product you see here is what he recommended. I think it's perfect.

The heart of the rifle is Jered's Genesis action that is built by Defiance. It has a Remington 700 footprint, but that's where the similarities stop. The Pic rail that runs along the top of the action is held in place by six 8-40 screws and two pins. The base attaches firmly to the action yet is also

The Manners MCS TF-1 stock has a "no-profile" hinge that is impossible to break and is hidden inside the grip. This clean, robust design makes the rifle extremely portable.

choose what components to use on this rifle. I'd never heard of Huber triggers before I shot a Paragon, so I was skeptical of putting one in this rifle. Like many readers, once I know what I like, I usually stick with it. Especially when I'm spending my money.

The trigger from Huber Concepts is amazing. I've shot some nice triggers in my life, but when my finger first touched the shoe, I paused to take a closer look. The black shoe is melted and bears no sharp edges. It is extremely comfortable, and firing the trigger was a treat. Mine is set up as a single stage, and it is exceptionally crisp with no creep. This one breaks at just over two pounds.

The barrel is from Broughton and is a 5.8 contour unique to American Precision Arms. Broughton makes excellent stainless steel barrels that are button rifled and very accurate. The Broughton barrels are so accurate that Jered guarantees quarter MOA for three shots on his .223 and .308 Paragon models. This type of guarantee would be impossible with anything other than a premium barrel.

The Manners MCS-TF1 stock is featured on this Paragon. Manners builds high-quality fiberglass stocks that are known to handle abuse well. For a long time their webpage showed a truck parked on one of their stocks. The TF1 is a great choice if you're looking for a stock that folds into a compact package for transport, has a forend that works both on the bags and fits comfortably in the support hand, and has an adjustable

removable should the base ever be damaged. The base also has a 30-MOA cant that makes it ideal for really long-range shooting.

The bolt is machined from one piece and bears Jered's fingerprints also. The extractor is of the M16 style, a much improved extractor over the factory Remington type because it grabs a lot more of the case before trying to

pull it out of the chamber. Jered also moved the ejector's location inside the bolt to ensure more positive ejection of the rounds. With the typical configuration, empty cases can sometimes fall back into the action if opened slowly. They then need to be fished out by hand.

The trigger is from Huber and reminds me why I'm glad I let Jered

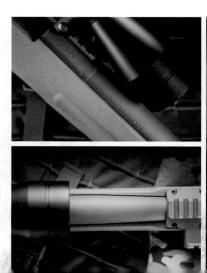

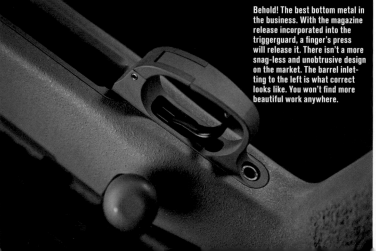

Behold! The best bottom metal in the business. With the magazine release incorporated into the triggerguard, a finger's press will release it. There isn't a more snag-less and unobtrusive design on the market. The barrel inletting to the left is what correct looks like. You won't find more beautiful work anywhere.

APA PARAGON

TYPE	Bolt action, long
CALIBER	.300 Winchester Magnum
CAPACITY	5, 10 rds.
BARREL	24 in.
OVERALL LENGTH	46 in. (extended), 36 in. (folded)
WEIGHT	13.1 lbs.
STOCK	Manners MCS-TF1
LENGTH OF PULL	13.5 in.
FINISH	FDE Cerakote
TRIGGER	Huber Concepts
SIGHTS	None
SAFETY	Two-position
MSRP	$6,840
MANUFACTURER	American Precision Arms 706-367-8881 americanprecisionarms.com

APA's "Little Jimmy" muzzlebrake took all of the recoil out of firing the rifle. It, too, is one of Jered's designs and is the author's first choice for muzzlebrakes when not shooting with a suppressor.

Jered's bottom metal takes Accuracy International magazines. An industry standard for any custom-built rifle, AI's magazines fed flawlessly and stand up well to abuse.

cheekpiece. It represents my first choice for a rifle built in .300 Win. Mag. because it's substantial enough to shoot comfortably in the prone (which is where I'll be when I want to shoot far) but not so big as to rule out positional shooting. It's a tough balance to strike, but the Manners TF1 does it well.

Great rifle components only combine for a superb rifle when someone who knows what he's doing assembles them. In this Jered excels. After I shot the rifle to test it for accuracy, I took it apart to have a look at the bedding job. It's beautiful. Proper bedding is crucial for accuracy because it's the only place where the barreled action contacts the stock (which is what we hold on to). It is the critical junction between the shooter and the working parts of the rifle. The bedding job is flawless and smooth with seating marks atop the pillars in perfect alignment with the bore's axis.

RANGE TIME

The load I wanted to use in the Paragon had Hornady's 208 A-MAX. I love its BC and its weight, so I had some loaded up for the range. The 208 A-MAX has that secant or flat ogive that makes the bullet temperamental. After some load development, I fired several groups with the A-MAX and

liked what I saw.

The Paragon comes with a quarter-MOA guarantee when chambered in .223 and .308. These are common calibers, and match ammo from numerous manufacturers is very high quality. The guarantee is also for three-shot groups.

My groups were five shots at 100 yards using handloads and a bullet that either loves or hates your rifle. This .300 Win. Mag. A-MAX handload was a match for the Paragon. The smallest group measured .51 inch, and the group average was .57 inch.

I'm usually good for half-MOA shooting if the rifle and ammo are up to it. Smaller than that and I need to be having a good day no matter how impressive the rifle and ammo. After shooting the Paragon I got the distinct impression that the rifle was more accurate than I was.

WINNERS AND LOSERS

While I love the .338 Lapua Magnum and still desire to own "one more," I think that most long-range shooters (myself included) will be better served by the .300 Winchester Magnum. The

ammo for the .300 is much more readily available, actions and stocks that fit them are more common, and even with a steep price point like the one found on the APA Paragon, .300 Win. Mag. rifles are less expensive than their .338 Lapua counterparts.

Once we start looking at the cost of ammo and its components, the .300 Win. Mag. really pulls away from the .338 Lapua. Ammo is cheaper, bullets are cheaper, and the .300 Win. Mag. only uses about 75 percent of the powder than the .338 does. When we load with the Hornady 208 A-MAX and

the 230 Berger, we also have bullets that give us what all but the best .338-caliber bullets do at a fraction of the price.

We can get a rifle in .300 Win. Mag. for about two-thirds of what a comparable model would cost in .338 Lapua Mag., the ammo costs half as much, and the .300 only has about two-thirds of the recoil. All these figures combine to form a compelling argument of why all of our wallets and shoulders prefer the .300 over the .338.

The Paragon I tested in .300 Win. Mag. represents the best that money

can buy from a man who has been building me rifles for several years. If you have some time, I encourage you to visit the APA website and watch the torture-testing videos where Jered abuses his $6,000 rifle. It'll make you a little sad to see a fine rifle treated this way, but you'll also get to see first-hand what kind of product comes from premium components and a skilled builder. Combine the .300 Win. Mag. with the Paragon, and we create a rifle that I'd shoot and enjoy more than any .338 Lapua.

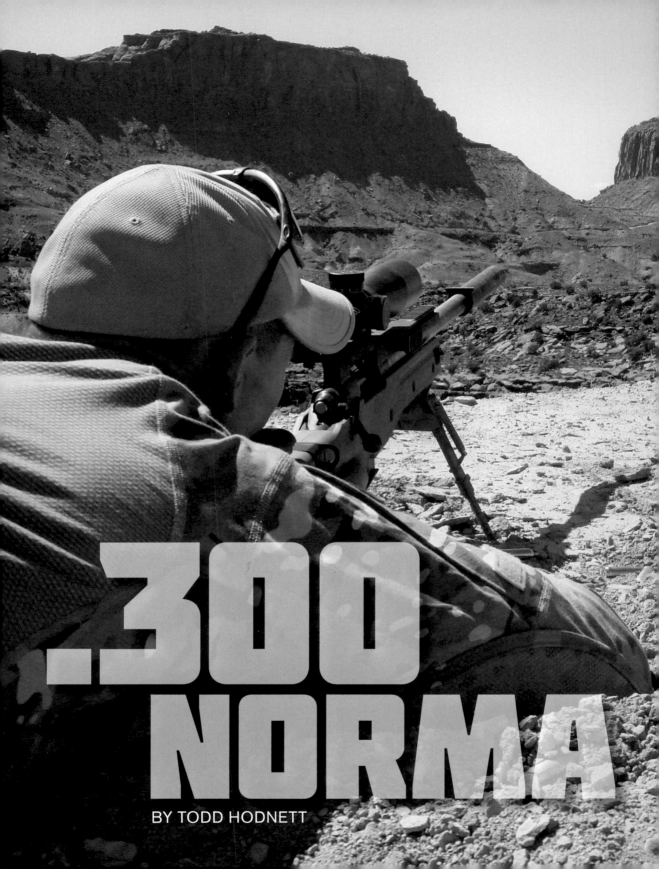

.300 NORMA

BY TODD HODNETT

IS THIS EVERYONE'S LONG-RANGE SOLUTION?

I am a huge fan of the .338 Lapua and have been an avid long-range hunter with this caliber for years. My two sons and I have taken game well beyond 1,000 meters and even some shots beyond 1,500 meters. The .338 LM has proven itself to me that it is highly capable of taking these types of shots. As a long-gun trainer for our boys going overseas, this sort of thing is what I do for a living—and it's my passion. So when I was looking for the next caliber option, I took a look at the .300 Norma.

I met cartridge designer Jimmy Sloan at the SHOT Show, and he explained the capabilities of the .300 Norma. I was very interested, but I really didn't want another barrel burner, so I watched as a few of my friends started playing with this caliber. They were amazed at the accuracy they were getting and how flat it was. I had a chance to shoot with a friend who owned a rifle in .300 Norma, and I was surprised while watching the trace. This new caliber had my attention.

When Berger came out with its new 230-grain, .30-caliber hybrid bullet, I was blown away at its .743 BC. I knew then that this was the bullet for my .300 Norma project. I was hoping the heavier bullet would give me the advantages in ballistics that I was looking for while allowing me to push it at a speed that would not burn out the barrel so quickly.

I called Preston Pritchett, owner of Surgeon Rifles, and placed my order for the rifle, ordering a 1:8-inch-twist barrel for it from Broughton. I am a fan of fast twist rates, so let's look at this very important component. Here are some considerations: barrel length and twist rate, long VLD-type bullets, heavier VLD-type bullets and shorter barrels may require a faster twist. I have tested this on several occasions and found the same answer with each test. In my opinion, the Greenhill Formula is a little outdated. Even though it may work for some types of bullets and some types of shooting, I believe we need much faster twist rates for extended long-range shots. This gives us better-retained gyroscopic stability as the bullet is reaching transonic flight and into subsonic flight, thus, better grouping capabilities as well as less loss of BC due to loss of stability. I even had a 1:7.8-inch twist on a .308. This was another Surgeon rifle, and it was one of the most accurate rifles I have ever seen.

Even though I expected the possibility of precision and possible large groups at 100, I was more concerned with grouping capability at 800 meters and beyond. Not only did this gun shoot sub-half-inch groups at 100, there were some groups so good that they measured out to be sub-quarter-inch. We used this gun in a military test that I was shooting, and the first 18 of 20 shots were in a four-inch group at 1,000 meters. So you can appreciate my love for fast twist.

Shorter barrels are also a big favorite of mine. I usually go for 20-inch barrels on my bolt guns because of a test that we did on the .338 Lapua in which we tested barrels from 18 to 27 inches. Since then, I have always shot 20-inch barrels on all my bolt guns.

However, this gun was being made for a couple of reasons: The first and foremost was for extreme long-range hunting. I was hoping this new caliber would prove itself worthy, and my next gun would be a 20 inch with a medium-weight barrel for a true hunting-weight rifle. For this rifle, however, I had to remove variables, so I tested it with a 26-inch barrel. This would test my super-fast twist, and the next step will be the barrel length.

Now let's start the comparison with a current requirement for the PSR contract or your next long-range hunting rifle. We'll compare the .300 Norma with the 230-grain Berger and a .338 Lapua with the 250-grain Scenar and the 300-grain Sierra as well as the current .300 Win. Mag. with both 190- and 220-grain Sierra bullets and the 230-grain Berger tactical bullet that is shorter and has slightly less BC.

All atmospherics will be at 70 degrees with a 27.0 station pressure and 50 percent humidity.

When I compare calibers for long-range work, there are several different points that should be looked at: ranges of transonic and subsonic flight, elevation holds of 1,000 meters and one mile (1,609 meters), 10-mph wind holds for 1,000 meters and one mile, remaining energy and remaining velocity for 1,000 meters and one mile.

To break down this information, let's look at the transonic range. As you can see in the chart, everything is really close here. The transonic portion of flight is important, as it lets you see how far your algorithm is working before it incurs transonic shockwaves. This is commonly thought of as the effective range of a weapons system.

Subsonic is still pretty tight, with the 250-grain .338 dragging a bit behind, though still subsonic well past a mile, and this is an important indicator as to how far your algorithm will work.

PERFORMANCE COMPARISON CHART

Load	Transonic Range (meters)	Subsonic Range (meters)	Elevation Hold 1,000m (mils)	Elevation Hold 1 mile (mils)	10mph Wind Holds 1,000m (mils)	10mph Wind Holds 1 mile (mils)	Remaining Energy 1,000m (ft-lbs)	Remaining Energy 1 mile (ft-lbs)	Remaining Velocity 1,000m (fps)	Remaining Velocity 1 mile (fps)
.300 Norma 230-grain Berger (.743 BC)	1,540	1,910	7.55	17.07	1.39	2.61	1,625	854	1,784	1,293
.338 Lapua 250-grain Scenar (.675 BC)	1,435	1,770	7.60	17.75	1.53	2.92	1,823	907	1,728	1,219
.338 Lapua 300-grain Sierra (.778 BC)	1,545	1,935	7.82	17.61	1.37	2.56	2,077	1,123	1,766	1,298
.300 Win. Mag. 190-grain Sierra (.533 BC)	1,170	1,440	8.13	21.11	2.01	3.92	975	458	1,520	1,042
.300 Win. Mag. 220-grain Sierra (.640 BC)	1,340	1,660	8.01	19.10	1.67	3.19	1,334	653	1,653	1,156
.300 Win. Mag. 230-grain Berger (.714 BC) ("tactical" 230-gr. for overall length)	1,470	1,830	7.76	17.76	1.47	2.78	1,544	794	1,739	1,247

The elevation holds are close as well, with the .300 Norma being the flatter choice.

The 10-mph wind hold in mils is really important, and these are close, but the Norma and the 300-grain .338 LM are the winners, with close to one MOA and nearly two MOA over its competitors. This is a big win, because wind is why we miss at long range, and this is a definite advantage. Notice the Berger 230 grain is holding its own in the .300 Win. Mag. because of its high BC.

The remaining energy is good on all and adequate for the job, but the .338 300-grain bullet really steps out here as the clear winner. There are a lot of people who tend to not look at remaining energy, but I still am interested in it. It is not one of my determining factors. We have killed pigs at more than a mile with .308s, which had only 283 ft-lbs of remaining energy at that point. The bullet went all the way through.

The remaining velocity is important, as we derive a lot of information from this number. As you can see, there are no real winners here; they all perform fairly evenly. The .300 Win. Mag. in the 190- and 220-grain versions are falling behind.

The .300 Norma I used in this comparison is one that I have, and these are the performance parameters of that weapon along with results from a .338 that I have shot on numerous occasions. I know that Berger has a 230-grain bullet with a .743 BC, and I have been told that I can load this to 3,000 fps.

Now let's compare those numbers. Let's talk about the downside. The caliber is not as mature when it comes to extreme long-range engagements when looking at options of bullets for different require-

ments. We need AP, expansion, ball and target ammo as well as the payload ability to handle a Raufoss-type capability for a strike indicator, and even the 300-grain is proving to be a stretch, so the 230 grain may not be enough. I know we have these types of bullets in the .308 calibers, but most don't meet the extended range requirement.

Now the upside. The caliber is .308, so it is super stable. The ammo can be bought at Black Hills and is cheaper than .338 and will be cheaper to handload. A good brake would be nice on either system. Due to the high BC and the lighter-weight bullet, the combination makes for a fast, flat-shooting rifle with performance that rivals the competitors of this field. Its performance proves it is really

Two soldiers shoot at a target so far away, it's invisible to the naked eye. This is typical of some of the shots they're required to make in Afghanistan.

Transonic Range (meters)	Subsonic Range (meters)	Elevation Hold 1,000m (mils)	1 mile (mils)	10mph Wind Holds 1,000m (mils)	1 mile (mils)	Remaining Energy 1,000m (ft-lbs)	1 mile (ft-lbs)	Remaining Velocity 1,000m (fps)	1 mile (fps)
1,635	2,005	6.85	15.49	1.30	2.46	1,788	936	1,874	1,357

As you can see, this combination is a clear winner in all departments but remaining energy. Loading this bullet properly may require one of the newer magazines that are four-plus inches in overall length. You can see why this new contender is making a big splash in the long-range world. These are really good numbers.

From Left to Right: .300 Win Mag, .300 Norma, .338 Lapua Mag

close to the .338 300 grain but still falls short in remaining energy. This is the only point that really sets them apart. But when we push the .300 Norma in its capabilities, it may actually win in all other comparisons and not just be equal.

A quick breakdown for reloaders: The overall length on the ammo from Black Hills is 3.595 inches. I am not sure of the powder Black Hills is using, but my friends tell me Retumbo, St. Marks and H1000 work really well. I know I can push the bullet faster, but I really like my dope. These are my holds:

200 = .3	**300** = .7	**400** = 1.4
500 = 2.2	**600** = 3	**700** = 4
800 = 5	**900** = 6	**1,000** = 7

This makes for an easy range card to set to memory. My actual holds may be off by .1 mil at a couple of ranges, but I can work with that. One of the positives of a muzzle velocity that is not too fast is the potential for barrel life extension. Maybe this one won't be a barrel burner.

Remember to put a level on your scope when shooting extreme long range. Remember that just 2.5 degrees of cant will shift your impact .5 mil at 1,000 meters. When shooting past 1,000 meters, this becomes extremely important. Another important factor is the change in temperature as the day goes on. The small changes we see in temperature from hour to hour may seem inconsequen-

tial—and, truthfully, they may be at short ranges—but when you start shooting well over 1,000 meters, these small changes can make a huge difference. Even a 13-degree swing can give you a .3-mil shift at one mile. This is close to 19 inches, so you can see the issue. Understand the effects that temperature has on density altitude and how it affects the elevation holds when engaging far targets.

All in all, the .300 Norma is a great new option for the long-range world, however, our other choices are no slouches. Whether you choose the .300 Norma, the .338 Lapua, or the .300 Win. Mag. with the new 230-grain Berger bullet (always a good caliber choice, and with the extra performance we are getting out of the Berger it is now really amazing), do your research and get to the range.

Don't let other people put their limits on you. Long-range shooting is a great hobby, art and lifelong passion. And it is extremely fun.

The author sets up to shoot his test rifle. The Surgeon-built rifle is exceptionally well made and features a Broughton barrel and an Accuracy International chassis/stock.

SETTING UP THE
7.62MM SNIPER SYSTEM

DESIGNING THE RIFLE TO MAKE EVERY SHOT COUNT.

BY SGM Kyle Lamb (Ret.)
PHOTOS BY Mark Fingar

Here the bipod is used to gain improved stability while using cover. Pressure is pushed from the rear of the gun into the wall, helping to control recoil.

Photo by Mark Fingar

These days there are many choices in the gas-operated 7.62mm sniper system world, which sometimes makes it confusing as you begin your quest for the perfect setup. I have spent plenty of my own money for those lessons learned, so hopefully you won't have to.

There are a few tricky parts and accessories that attract attention, but my intention is to always have a rifle that is reliable, accurate, simple and lightweight. Simple is relative. For my use, simple is a system that translates nicely from the M4-type carbine to the sniper system. Not only are the controls similar, but my accessories will be identical or extremely close. In the past these systems were available, but weight and reliability left us wanting. Thankfully, we now have a few choices that can cut the mustard in the light-weight sniping world. My lightweight choice is the LaRue PredatAR. This system is truly revolutionary in the fact that you don't need a weight belt or a series of P90X workouts to be able to move effectively in a tactical environment. Running-and-gunning with a sniper system briefs well in the Team Room, but if you are blowing snot bubbles by the time you need to take a shot due to the weight of your rifle, well, that just won't work. At the very least it will make you less effective when your mates need you most.

More than just a little thought should go into the selection process of your 7.62 Sniper System. The evaluation of the platform itself is obviously the most important, a reliable system that will work well with the ammunition you choose to employ or the ammunition that your department or unit issues. I normally shoot 175-grain M118LR ammunition. As this ammo launches a 175-grain Sierra MatchKing bullet, I must ensure that the twist fits the bullet. In this case I prefer the 1:11 twist. Actually, I have chosen the LaRue PredatAR, which has a 1:11.25 twist. This ammunition is used for two reasons. First, it is the issue ammunition for many of the military folks we train at VTAC. Second, it is very accurate. If I decide to take the same system into the hunting field—for the four-legged type of animal, that is—I jam my Magpul magazines with the Hornady 165-grain GMX load. The LaRue PredatAR is in love with this ammunition. If you haven't checked out the GMX bullet, it performs superbly when shooting through glass or into flesh. These bullets are gilding metal, which equates to a smoother bullet than solid copper and will result in less fouling.

Now that twist is confirmed to fit the weight and profile of our selected projectiles, we should look at the operating system. I am not really picky other than the rifle needs to be light, reliable and, often overlooked, ergonomically correct. Ergonomics of the AR may not be for everyone, but for those of us who cut our teeth in the military with the M16, it feels pretty natural. Reliability is an easy fix these days, with most manufacturers answering the mail. However, light weight is a completely different issue. Here is where the LaRue PredatAR smokes everyone, at 7¾ pounds for a 16.1-inch-barreled 7.62 semiautomatic rifle. This equals a very attractive package for those who will be carrying more than shooting. If you plan to lie on your belly and shoot paper all day, get the behemoth blasters with heavy barrels and gadgets galore. Now that I have hung up the uniform, I spend several months a year in the mountains with a rifle, either hunting or teaching high-angle shooting and pack-animal courses. Some days are spent backpack hunting where extra weight can determine whether you get to your prey. Other times I am riding a horse and the extra weight is easily carried by the horse when the rifle is in a scabbard, but if you have to sling the rifle it can crush you after a few long days hanging on for dear life. Even if you are tooling around on an ATV or snow machine, no matter the mode

of transportation, weight matters. The amount of abuse I'd receive from a heavy rifle just isn't worth it for the amount of shooting I will be doing. So, if you are like me and will be moving and shooting, light weight is the ticket.

Part of the weight-loss program for the LaRue PredatAR is the removable railed free-float system, which allows you to have a modular system that can be changed to fit your mission. In the past I have often been mocked for choosing this type of system. Now it is standard fare for most rifle manufacturers. Funny how things change.

Since semiauto is the selected system, we also need a trigger that is reliable for the operation of this rifle. LaRue has selected the Geissele trigger, which works out well since that would be the trigger I would choose regardless for this type of setup.

PROPERLY ADJUSTED STOCK

MANY TIMES DURING classes I find students shooting with their stocks collapsed or at least in the too-short category. An easy way to get the proper length of pull is to place the buttstock in the crook of your arm at the elbow, then grab the pistol grip. If it is natural, you are close. If you have to bend your wrist or reach for the pistol grip, the length is wrong. Once it is adjusted, you may need to collapse one more click if shooting with body armor.

Tools of the modern sniper rifle from bottom left: Torx wrench set, Leupold lens pen, small level, half-inch wrench for detaching rings from base, T-handle with 65 inch-pounds torque wrench and Wheeler's FAT adjustable torque driver with bits.

Photos by Mark Fingar

OBSTRUCTED OBJECTIVE LENS

UNLIKE IRON SIGHTS, magnified optics are magic. OK, maybe not magic, but you can get away with a lot more. One example is shooting around obstructions such as through steps or from drain holes in the parapet of a building. If you look at the hole and there is enough room for the barrel and a small portion of your optic, you might be good to go. Get into position, and see what it looks like. More times than not, the target may be slightly hazy, but you will be able to see well enough to engage easily out to 400 yards.

OK, the rifle is good to go. What else will we need? Optics: Leupold Mark 6 3-18X—period. There isn't a scope on the market that has the pedigree of the Mark 6. Built to the rigid specifications of U.S. Army Special Operators by a highly respected U.S. manufacturer, this glass is 11 ounces lighter, even with a 34mm main tube, as well as 1½ inches shorter than its competitors. Ounces make pounds for sure in this case, and I don't want to carry the 11 ounces without any noticeable enhancements. There

are several reticles you can choose from. My favorite is the H58 that is a gridded milliradian pattern that makes hold-offs a breeze. The Mark 6 also has a pinch-and-turn locking elevation dial that is calibrated to .1 mil. This system is intuitive and only requires you to pinch the turret and turn, no pulling up or pushing down. The windage is covered, as it should be on a 7.62 sniper system, no accidental adjustments while fast-roping or crawling. This is key. If you are required to shoot long range with the H58 reticle, you will see no distortion at the edges of the glass.

Optics and rifle make a nice package, but to truly get your money's worth out of the system there are a few enhancements that I won't leave home without. First would be a good weapon-mounted light. I use a VTAC-L4 that is made by SureFire. I prefer to use the protected push button versus a pressure pad, which ensures that there won't be a white-light Accidental Discharge (AD) while moving into my Final Firing Position (FFP) or during normally required crawling and climbing. I mount the SureFire in a VTAC light mount. Made from glass-filled nylon, it is also light and rugged. Next would be Back Up Iron Sights (BUIS). I have found

Photos by Mark Fingar

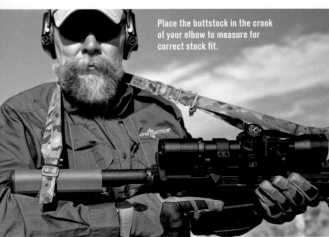

Place the buttstock in the crook of your elbow to measure for correct stock fit.

Although obnoxious, the muzzlebrake is nice for recoil control as well as allowing for the connection of a SureFire suppressor. The bipod can be used as a vertical grip for CQB operations. A good sling allows for the operator to quickly stow the rifle and climb if needed.

Photos by Mark Fingar

the Troy DOA is one tough sight that can stand up to my daily abuse. Some believe backup sights are not needed for this type of setup. All I would say is, "You never know." If your optic were to fail, you can't simply transition to your sidearm and make a 300-yard shot.

For sound and flash suppression, I favor the SureFire muzzlebrake, which adapts to the SureFire suppressor. This system will help keep you on target during rapid-fire situations and makes attaching and removing your suppressor extremely easy. Using the suppressor with full-up ammunition will not make the rifle completely quiet, although it will help to confuse the enemy as to where the shot came from and help to eliminate muzzle flash. Either way, the bad guys should be confused, and that is what we are after.

A couple of other ancillary pieces of kit that are a must on the 7.62 rifle are the sling and the bipod. Of course, I use the VTAC MK-2 Padded sling or the VTAC Sniper sling, which is essentially the same setup with the addition of a quick-release cuff, which comes in handy in certain shooting situations. This sling allows you to use it as a shooting aid and can be quickly tightened to hold the rifle securely on your back when climbing.

The bipod I use is the Harris. Although not very sexy, it is extremely reliable and not very heavy. I have tried a few others but keep coming back to this setup. More notable is the use of the bipod and where you attach it. There are a few tricks I have learned along the way, one of which is to turn the bipod backward so the legs point to the rear when collapsed for rural movement. This will alleviate the issues of vegetation continuously opening or grabbing your bipod legs. Once in position, you can easily disconnect the bipod and turn it around if you see fit. Additionally, I prefer to keep the bipod in a position closer to the magazine of the rifle when operating in an urban environment. By simply moving the bipod to the rear six to 10 inches, you are able to transition much faster from target to target as well as elevate or depress the rifle when shooting over parapets or from rooftops. This also puts the bipod closer to the center of gravity, making the rifle feel a little lighter. If you haven't tried this, I highly recommend you give it a go. You will immediately see a difference in the amount of movement you can get from this simple change.

The last bit of advice I would give you as a former Special Forces sniper would be this: Get on the range and shoot. Don't lie down and shoot groups. Get a solid zero, then shoot from realistic positions. And shoot a lot.

The best way to learn is by doing.

Having a good bipod that can be quickly moved closer to the rear of the gun comes in handy. This is especially true when shooting from non-standard platforms.

PRECISION SHOOTING
WITH A TRIPOD

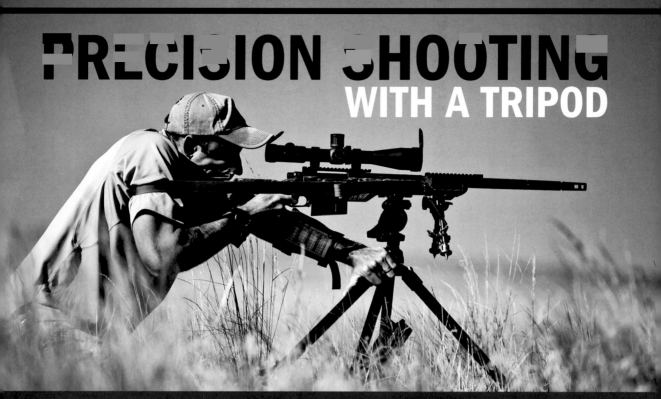

A SNIPER'S THREE-LEGGED BEST FRIEND.
BY CAYLEN WOJCIK

As a sniper, I can recall countless situations when otherwise optimal final firing positions were scrapped due to an inability to construct a solid supported shooting platform. Perfect-world prone positions are a rarity in any real-world scenario. In either a green-side or urban environment, the ability to obtain a suitable position hinged on whether I could acquire an obstacle-free line of sight to the target while remaining covert, as well as maintain a sustainable shooting support.

Don't get me wrong; old-fashioned fieldcraft always prevailed if the situation permitted the construction of a shooting position without compromising the mission through sound or movement. The archived photos of positions built from 550 cord, cargo straps, bungee cords and the ever-present rigger's tape still make me chuckle, not from the apparent lunacy and jerry-rigging, but merely from knowing what I know now about using such a simple piece of gear as a tripod. The painstaking hours spent

of the past are now replaced by using one incredibly versatile, simple tool that takes seconds to employ with deadly effectiveness in the hands of a trained sniper. The tripod is the only tool that allows the sniper to have a guaranteed shooting support wherever he goes.

The camera tripod comes in many flavors, and the end user should take a careful look at his needs before selecting a model that best suits the end requirement. As with most equipment, the "buy once, cry

see students in Magpul Dynamic's Precision Rifle Operations classes attempt to make a Walmart special work, and it generally ends in frustration and ultimately lost training value. Manfrotto has been the go-to brand of tripods for snipers, and there are myriad options. Bottom line: Look for sturdy legs that offer rapid height adjustments and the ability to widen the base of the tripod through adjusting the angle of one leg independent of the others. This feature will also allow the shooter to utilize the tripod in uneven-terrain situations. Carbon fiber models offer substantial savings in weight while maintaining rigidity, which is something to consider if you intend to move any amount of distance while carrying your gear. However, as with everything carbon fiber, those models are going to hit the pocketbook. Aluminum models will suffice for most.

Once the tripod has been selected, the next thing to look at is a ball head, or the interface between the top of the tripod and the gear you intend to mount to the tripod. I want gear that serves multiple purposes, is simple and is as lightweight as possible. The more points of movement a ball head has, the more intricate it is to operate and, of course, the more potential points of failure there are.

How to mount the rifle to the tripod? We've come a long way from fashioning a section of cut-in-half 3-inch PVC pipe to the tripod head and wrapping it with foam padding and rigger's tape. There are two methods I have seen widely used within the sniper community. The first is the LaRue Tactical Picatinny rail interface that is found in the SPOTR kit. This little gem allows you to directly mount a rifle that has sections of rail in the 6 o'clock position to the tripod. Most semiautos and some bolt-action chassis systems offer the ability to mount sections of rail in locations of the end-user's choice. The other option is the HOG Saddle from Shadow Tech. Fellow Marine Sniper Joshua Stabler has created a truly innovative product that allows the shooter

to mount the rifle to the tripod through a simple clamping mechanism. Another key bonus is the rubber padding that cradles the rifle, which also dramatically absorbs felt recoil, helping the shooter maintain the crucial second sight picture after follow-through. This is now my go-to piece of gear, and it is always with my rifle and tripod.

NATURAL POINT OF AIM

Now that the gear issues have been worked out, we need to focus on what is actually going to help us consistently put rounds on target. As with any shooting discipline, strict, Gestapo-like adherence to the fundamentals of marksmanship is the only true recipe to establishing consistency. In the world of precision shooting, the ability to acquire and maintain a natural point of aim (NPA) is absolutely paramount to success, even more so when attempting to engage a small target at distance with a tripod. At the end of the day, you have to learn how to get the rifle to do what you want it to, all while maintaining a relaxed body position. This is easier said than done, and it is often a point of contention among students. When it's mastered and the little light bulb switches on, you will become unstoppable,

On today's battlefield, shots are rarely taken from the prone. A tripod offers a ready-made shooting platform that works in almost any battle environment.

Manfrotto 055CXPRO3 Tripod

MATERIALS	Carbon fiber and magnesium
MAXIMUM HEIGHT	68.9 in.
MINIMUM HEIGHT	4.5 in.
FOLDED LENGTH	25.6 in.
LOAD CAPACITY	17.6 lbs.
WEIGHT	3.64 lbs.
MSRP	$534
MANUFACTURER	Manfrotto 201-818-9500 manfrotto.us

Shooter's Tech HOG Saddle

TYPE	Rifle rest
MATERIALS	CNC aluminum, stainless steel hardware
FINISH	Hard anodized
WEIGHT	16 oz.
MSRP	$309
MANUFACTURER	Shadow Tech 913-602-0665 hogsaddle.com

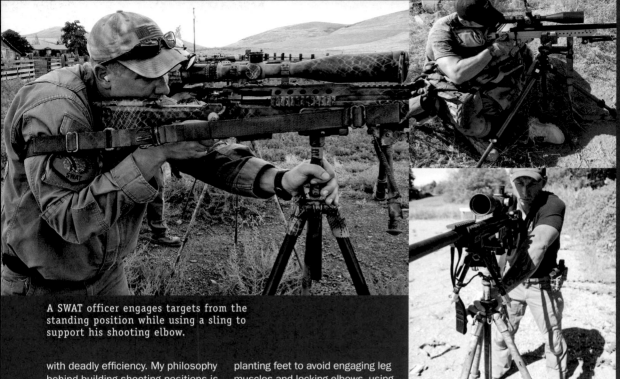

A SWAT officer engages targets from the standing position while using a sling to support his shooting elbow.

with deadly efficiency. My philosophy behind building shooting positions is simple: Adhere to the fundamentals, and all will be right with your world as you see it through your sights. With tripods, some little tricks and tweaks are necessary to squeak out every last bit of support you can from them.

Natural point of aim is something I harp on incessantly when shooting from positions other than prone. Yes, NPA is crucial to any position, but prone is pretty easy in the grand scheme of things and gets downright boring after a while. In a compromised shooting position, NPA is essentially going to allow the shooter to keep his point of aim within the constraints of the target, hopefully inside a smaller spot within the intended target, minimizing reticle movement. The only way this can occur is to achieve muscular relaxation through supporting the body's points of articulation with bones or other available means. A conscious effort on behalf of the shooter to mentally check every portion of his body to ensure relaxation as well as support is necessary for success when shooting from a tripod. Such things include locking knees and firmly planting feet to avoid engaging leg muscles and locking elbows, using arms or packs to support the body while not engaging core muscles, and utilizing slings where available to secure every part of the body and firearm with some sort of support.

Once the shooting position and a rough point of aim have been established, it's time to check the NPA. Going through a mental checklist is the only way you can be truly honest with yourself, and it's the only way you're going to consistently put bullets where you want them to go. Close your eyes, and go through all the points of support: feet planted, knees locked (if you're standing), legs relaxed, spine and upper body supported, core relaxed, nonshooting elbow locked and supported, shooting elbow supported (with a knee or sling, or both), and hit your respiratory pause. Open your eyes, and observe where the crosshairs are. If they're not on target, that's OK. Take a look at what they're pointed at, and see how rock-solid they are. Guess why? It's that whole natural point-of-aim thing coming together.

Top right: This student utilizes his pack as support for his upper body while in a seated position. His shooting elbow is supported on the pack, making the best use of all available points of contact.

Bottom right: The author demonstrates proper positioning of his nonshooting hand and arm. His elbow is locked, creating bone support, and his hand is placed to evenly distribute the forward load among all three tripod legs.

Now we need to get the rifle to do what we want it to do, and that's to put that same rock-solid point of aim we see down onto the target. We do this by making micromovements with our body. A little goes a long way, so practice to get the feel of what's what. Keep checking your NPA after making your adjustments, and when you're satisfied with the stability, apply

Clip-On Night Vision Accessory

"Z-Rail"

Ball Head

Tripod

Observation Telescope

"I-Rail"

Tripod Column

LaRue Tactical SPOTR Kit

> **"IF YOU DID IT ALL CORRECTLY, YOU'LL BE PLEASANTLY SURPRISED WHEN THE RIFLE RECOVERS FROM RECOIL AND YOUR SIGHT PICTURE IS PRETTY DARN CLOSE TO WHERE IT WAS WHEN THE SHOT BROKE."**

proper trigger control, follow through, and reacquire your sight picture. If you did it all correctly, you'll be pleasantly surprised when the rifle recovers from recoil and your sight picture is pretty darn close to where it was when the shot broke. You'll be able to spot your impact all on your own. Observers — who needs them anyway?

STRAP UP

Some other tricks for squeezing every last bit of support out of your system are there for the taking, and their use is completely dependent on your mission and the time available. Starting with the nonshooting arm, I developed a technique while training with some Marines. While shooting from tripods, I noticed that the rifle sling wasn't being used in the traditional sense; it

was hanging free. I realized that the only portion of my body that wasn't supported was my shooting elbow. By rerouting the sling to the strong side, I slipped the sling behind my triceps and adjusted it so that when my shooting-hand grip was in place, the sling had tension on it. This accomplished two things, the first being that now my shooting elbow was supported and not flopping in the breeze. The other was that the rifle was now even more positively engaged in the pocket of my shoulder through the pull action created. This immediately proved to assist with recoil management and made a huge difference in self-impact spotting. This is a pretty quick way to use your sling in just about any position where the front of the rifle is supported.

If the shooter is going to be in position for a length of time, a simple cargo strap can be used to further support the rifle. By wrapping one end of the strap around the rifle's bipod or front sling attachment and routing the strap through the apex of the tripod and then attaching it to the shooter's belt, another triangle of support is created. This method is incredibly supportive in all the positions, most notably the standing. Consistent body shots at distances in excess of 1,100 yards are well within reach. Although extremely stable, this technique could possibly lead to issues in a situation where rapid egress from a

position is necessary. Think it through; make sure you can get out of it quickly before you become permanently attached to your rifle and tripod.

From a tactical standpoint, snipers who employ tripods make themselves even more efficient force multipliers, whether on the field of battle or in a homeland crisis. Tripods allow the sniper to use just about any position that is tactically feasible for the mission. The rapid, no-nonsense setup gets the sniper in position light-years faster than before, which means getting eyes on the battle space or crisis site faster. With the HOG Saddle, the sniper has the ability to orient his firearm in the most ready position possible next to being behind the glass, allowing him to better multitask with items such as observation, communications and possibly directing supporting arms. Movement is as simple as removing the rifle from the saddle, folding up the legs and stuffing it in your ruck. Shots are rarely taken from the prone, and the modern sniper should be taking advantage of every tool that can go in his proverbial toolbox. With the proper training, the tripod gives you an undeniable advantage, and when it's mastered, your rifle will never again go anywhere without one.

DELIBERATE SUBSURFACE HIDES

BY Cody Carroll   **PHOTOS BY** Shayla Manzara

BUILDING COMFORTABLE CONCEALMENT AND COVER.

Without a doubt, the most effective way to conceal a sniper or reconnaissance team is with a subsurface hide. The subsurface hide offers significant advantages over the surface-hide site. It can offer cover from small arms and indirect fire, concealment from five meters (or closer) and comfort for multi-day surveillance operations.

An amphibious reconnaissance team prepares to set up a deliberate subsurface hide.

The problems encountered with subsurface hides, whether deliberate or hasty, are that they take a significant amount of manpower and materials to construct. They must also be built within the hours of limited visibility, which, without rehearsals, can be fairly difficult. Also, you have to think about procuring materials that can support several hundred pounds of dirt. You don't want the team vulnerable to counter-reconnaissance, counter-snipers and tracking teams. In order to limit the amount of manpower and construction materials procured and mitigate the threat of tracking teams, the reconnaissance or sniper element should consider a deliberate subsurface hide.

All successful missions begin with detailed planning, and if you're planning on going below deck, employing the use of a so-called "mule team" and bringing some simple materials will save a lot of work in the long term. A mule team can be any element that supports the main effort by providing transportation of equipment and on-site manpower. The mule team should be familiar with sniper and reconnaissance operations and capable of handling its own security. They, too, must also be skilled in fieldcraft and patrol operations.

A subsurface hide kit will take a few hours of preparation to construct. If you're planning to have three men in the subsurface site, you will need two sheets of plywood. If you have less than three men, you only need one sheet of plywood. Plywood typically comes in 8x4-foot sheets. They'll need to be cut down into transportable pieces. Plywood should be cut width-wise into 2x4-foot strips. These panels will form the roof of your subsurface hide. You will also need to prepare the frame that these panels sit on. This can be done with eight-foot lengths of 2x4s. The 2x4s can be cut into four-foot sections and predrilled to be assembled on-site with bolts. The mule team can also carry the 2x4s intact. If you are building a three-man hide, which will have an eight-foot-by-eight-foot footprint, you will need five eight-foot 2x4s to support the structure. Two eight-foot 2x4s will support the outer edges, and three will run perpendicular to the outside edges and line up with the strips of plywood. If you are only building a two-man hide, you will only need the eight-foot 2x4s and three four-foot 2x4s. This may seem like a lot of material to bring on a patrol, and it is.

The alternative is to cut several dozen logs that are a minimum of four inches in diameter and transport them to the hide's construction site. The amount of time lost, security required and spoor that this creates is not practical for the tempo of most operations today. The addition of a four-man mule team can easily spread-load the 90-pound subsurface hide kit on four pack frames. Because this team should already have skills in sniper and reconnaissance operations, they can depart the area undetected after their job is done. They can also provide additional security during the construction of the site. A base layer of paint and texture should be added to the wood in advance of the mission. A coat of spray glue and vegetation, dirt or sand from your Area of Operations (AO) will camouflage the kit during transport.

Once the site is selected, construction should begin as soon as possible. This is where rehearsals pay great dividends. The team leader needs to first select the spot where the viewport must be. Once that is marked and the camera or observation equipment is placed, then the rest of the hide will be constructed around the viewport.

Before the first spade cuts into the earth, string a couple of bungee cords at about head level in front of the site. Then hang a poncho from them. This will serve to reflect any noise during construction and mask a lot of the movement that will be taking place. Precut lengths of eight-foot 550 cord that will mark the perimeter of the hide. Lay down multiple ponchos to the left and right of the site. This will keep dirt excavated during construction from spilling onto the ground. Remember, you don't want to leave anything on the ground after the sun is up that can give away the position. Carefully remove the topsoil, and place it onto your poncho. Take great care in this step, as this will be the last layer back onto your site when construction is complete.

Once the topsoil has been removed, put the 2x4s that will be on the outside into place, then the two middle 2x4s and screw one of the plywood strips into place. This will allow one man to dig and dump dirt on each side of the wood without clanking shovels together, and it will also minimize the amount of dirt you have to haul off to conceal. You should dig to the depth that you will be comfortable with, or to one that

Select a site that maximizes use of natural obstacles.

Work on opposite sides of the hide to minimize noise.

you have time to. I prefer to be able to sit up in a hide, but this will be mission and user dependent.

Once that section of plywood is at max capacity for dirt, add in another section and continue to pile the dirt directly onto the top of it until you have used all of your material and your hole is the correct depth to be occupied. Remember to designate an area to place tools and equipment when not in use. This will prevent you from accidently burying them or leaving some behind after the team has occupied.

Next, you will need to construct a frame for an escape hatch and cover it with netting. This will go on

the back end (opposite side of your view port) of your hide. Concurrently, apply spray glue to any exposed wood edges and rub them with dirt. At this point the hide is almost ready. Go ahead and replace that top layer of soil that you carefully removed and set to the side on the poncho.

Last, use some screen or a net of the right color to get rid of the contained shadow that your viewport is making.

It is important that no one disturbs the vegetation between the hide site and the objective during the construction phase. Get the surveillance team into the site, and conduct communications checks. If required, rig up a

The team selects a tentative site.

Predrilled parts for the kit secured with a sling rope for amphibious transport.

Photos by Shayla Manzara

"The mule team should be familiar with sniper and reconnaissance operations and capable of handling its own security."

Assemble the hide roof one piece at a time.

Ensure that the rear escape hatch is big enough to get out with your kit.

Use netting to help eliminate the shadow from the viewport.

camouflaged pulley system and some fishing line to a field-expedient long wire antenna, as radio communication from a subsurface site is often hard to do. This will allow the hide-site team to pull out their antennas from inside the hide during their communications windows. Satcom should be possible from below the escape hatch, as it is just netting covered with some light vegetation. Once the team is in and radio communication is established and checked, it is the team leader's responsibility to apply the final camouflage to the site before nautical dawn.

Construction of the deliberate subsurface site requires planning,

preparation and a lot of sweat equity. It may not be the solution for every mission, but in those cases where the extra cover and concealment are required, or if there isn't enough material in the area of operations to construct one, it's a logical solution. The kit is low cost and can be constructed and prepared before a deployment. It's not exactly light-weight, but with enough men, it can be broken down and the weight at that point is minimal. It also floats, so it can be an option for amphibious operations where teams can be on the beach for up to four days conducting surf reports and beach

reports before a major amphibious landing. The traditional method of constructing a subsurface hide site places the reconnaissance or sniper team at risk of compromise by forcing it to procure construction materials in the field. This creates trails from the procurement area directly to the hide. It requires too much security and creates a lot of noise. The deliberate subsurface hide kit mitigates these threats by preparing the major materials and packaging them into camouflaged and transportable sections before the mission begins.

UNDETECTED

CAMOUFLAGE IS STILL RELEVANT.
BY CAYLEN WOJCIK

When you think of a sniper, images of the scoped rifle and the ghillie suit come to mind almost immediately. The rifle is obvious, but the ghillie suit? What is that jumbled mess of cloth and burlap for? How does it conceal that guy and make him appear invisible? Well, it isn't a cloaking device, as we would all like to imagine. Much like a loaded gun, the ghillie suit is completely useless without a competent operator. The ghillie suit is merely a tool a sniper uses in order to accomplish his mission. Contrary to popular belief, the ghillie suit is rarely used by the operational sniper for reasons we'll be covering throughout this article. The ghillie is used more as an initial training tool to establish the key fundamentals or building blocks of camouflage, concealment and techniques of individual movement in the sniper trainee.

Without getting into too much history, the ghillie suit came from Scottish gamekeepers. These gamekeepers needed some sort of camouflage to break up their outline while counting herds of game animals on the barren landscape of the Scottish Highlands. The suit hasn't changed much since then. Aside from using modern base fabrics and textiles, snipers are still attaching shredded burlap and strips of tattered cloth to their suits. One thing that must be understood about the ghillie suit is that it isn't going to conceal the sniper without natural vegetation being incorporated into it. The burlap and fabric strips are only in place to assist in breaking up the wearer's outline, and the natural vegetation is the actual camouflage: "Natural veg is the edge." Too much burlap and cloth attached to the suit will actually hurt its effectiveness, as it will inhibit the use of the natural stuff.

The U.S. Marine Corps stalking program is unquestionably the most difficult aspect of Scout/Sniper School. With overall attrition rates in the 70 percent range, at least 80 percent of that number is a result of students falling victim to the stalking program. Stalking and camouflage are art forms, and they are traits one possesses naturally. The core principles and fundamentals of camouflage can be taught, as can the techniques of proper individual movement. However, when the boots hit the stalking lane and the call "under observation!" comes across the radio, you either have it or you don't. As instructors, we used to call it the "light bulb." Students who grew up hunting and more exposed to fieldcraft quickly showed competence. Others aren't so fortunate, and stalking becomes a dreaded evolution until that light bulb comes on. Once that bulb clicks, there really isn't anything that's going to stop that student as long as he does everything right. Those students who don't experience the light bulb moment become statistics.

For quite some time, the stalking program came under relentless fire from critics who cited it as an unnecessary skill. These critics were usually commanding officers who, after looking at attrition rates, decided that the program was too difficult to be reasonably passed by the average student. The concerns also left them wondering why they didn't have any qualified snipers. During my tenure as an instructor, this was a constant battle. We always fought back with the point that stalking trains the sniper in individual movement, techniques of camouflage and target indicators. All of the above are essential for a sniper's survival on the battlefield. Soon after the battlefield became more of an urban environment, commanders were also quick to point out that the graded stalking evolutions were not consistent with our current operational environment. The school's standard grading system was based on green-side environments using a ghillie suit as camouflage. I would always sadly shake my head at the bureaucracy.

What these commanders didn't understand was that the fundamentals remain the same regardless of the operational environment. Stalking gives the student a raw view of the importance of attention to detail and discipline. Essentially, effective camouflage and individual movement are the results of scrupulous attention to detail and the discipline displayed by the sniper. Watering down the program to see a decrease in attrition is only going to get snipers killed. Akin to asking a student of mechanics to tear down an engine without first understanding how to use a ratchet, you're setting up that student for failure. In the life of a sniper the ability to remain undetected is survival.

The physical act of stalking is moving yourself and all your mission-essential gear into a final firing position while remaining undetected. Generally, this is accomplished using a combination of camouflage and the proper techniques of individual movement for the given scenario. For snipers, compromise is mission failure. "Always assume you are under enemy observation" is a phrase that I never forget because it will keep me in the proper mental mindset to

maintain that level of attention to detail and discipline. Camouflage consists of many things, and this article isn't meant to dive into the most technical aspects of it.

I don't have a PhD, but I know and understand the principles. Camouflage is meant to disrupt the vision of an observer. This is accomplished by creating disruptive patterns (i.e., a ghillie suit) and crypsis, which means to blend with the background. The single largest mistake one makes when trying to

camouflage is not disrupting his outline. The human eye reacts differently as it attempts to discern objects at varying distances.

When attempting to identify an object, the eye will remove detail from the suspect object in order to create an outline. This is the major reason that most commercially available camouflage patterns aren't effective. They contain too much detail and are generally too dark in tone. This combination automatically creates an outline regardless of the lighting conditions. The wonderfully composed photos in magazine advertisements are perfectly set in environments that represent the pattern. This is obviously never the case for the real-world operator or hunter. Our brains are programmed to see outlines. One of the key principles of observation is to look for features that are not natural in the environment. The flat back of an elk moving through the predominantly vertical features of thick timber is an excellent example. The other common mistake is operators making themselves too dark in color. It is best to start with light colors, as you can always make something darker. Trying to make something dark into something light doesn't work out well.

The factors that usually get people into trouble while trying to remain undetected are improper

movement, improper camouflage and failing to keep an object in between themselves and the observer. Improper movement is generally classified as the stalker being in a position that is higher than the surrounding environment, thus creating an outline. Another threat is overhead movement. The stalker could well be low enough, but if he moves a piece of vegetation and causes it to move unnaturally, this will draw the observer's attention, and it goes downhill from there. The human eye is attracted to quick movements, especially in an environment where objects are largely stationary.

Improper camouflage can be classified as several things: shine, outline and contrast with the background. Shine can be as simple as sun glinting off a lens or metallic object or even an improperly camouflaged human face. Common grasses placed at angles outside the normal will also reflect sunlight. Outline is very simple, usually resulting in a combination of improper movement (too high) and lack of natural vegetation. The use of natural vegetation in the ghillie suit is what creates crypsis and causes the wearer to seem invisible. It is the key component of camouflage. As the stalker moves through one environment to another, he must stop and change out the natural vegetation to mimic his surroundings. He also needs to be aware of its color, as after it's cut, it will wilt and eventually die. This is also a form of improper camouflage. Contrast with the background is a concept that most people have difficulty with. Much like commercial camouflage, the stalker will fail to blend with his background, hence creating an outline. We can see clearly now that one mistake snowballs into many problems, hence the importance of mindset and discipline.

Something I always do if I'm stalking against observers is attempt to create a depth-perception problem for them. I use natural vegetation to make the front of my body look like the bush I'm hiding in (my foreground), then make the top of my head and shoulders look like my background. This effectively creates total crypsis through mimicry. The stalker can fine-tune his position by using counter-shading techniques. If you cast a shadow (you will), use some vegetation to break up the shadows that weren't there naturally.

So far we've beat up the green-side environment, but what about the urbanscape that we are mainly fighting in now? The same principles apply, just with different colors and patterns. The ghillie suit is in the kit bag and out comes the subdued and painted overwhites. Looking at the predominant colors of the operational environment, the sniper can create a disruptive pattern consisting of hard lines and shadows using khaki and yellow tones of spray paint. These hard lines blend seamlessly with the rubble and shadows cast in the urban environment. This is also an environment where the modern digital and mottled patterns work well. The light tones of the disruptive Multicam pattern blend well in the yellow and tan tones of the urban landscape. The USMC desert MARPAT works wonderfully when seasoned with a little sweat and grime. Utilizing the geometry of rooms and the resulting darkened corners will make it almost impossible to detect movement in an urban environment. Techniques of individual movement—see how this is all coming together even in an urban environment?

We can see from the preceding paragraphs that stalking and camouflage are a mindset and require the utmost levels of attention to detail. The controlled environment of school can create a false sense of security for the operator, though. Enter the operational environment, which is a 360-degree world. No more two-dimensional stalk lanes. Now we have trails, boot prints and sign deposited by our patrol. How do we mitigate these problems? This is where we enter the world of patrolling tactics. Most areas I operated in were rural agricultural regions. The farmers knew their property and were very perceptive of any irregularities. A boot print can effectively equal mission compromise. Humans aren't always the factor either. Stray dogs wreaked havoc on patrols. Their keen sense of smell and low-light eyesight made them formidable opponents in our quest to remain concealed. There is nothing more frustrating than having a half-dozen dogs bark at you for hours. A suppressed 9mm Sten was the weapon of choice, but you still had a dead dog to worry about. Compromise was around every corner.

We've seen that in order for the sniper to become proficient and remain undetected in all environments, he must first have a firm grasp on the fundamentals of camouflage and individual movement. Much like weapons manipulation and marksmanship, stalking for the sniper needs to become an unconscious competence. It's a skill that is honed every day through constant, meticulous attention to detail and discipline. For a sniper, compromise is mission failure. Period. Always assume you're under observation. Suffer patiently and patiently suffer.

PICK 'EM UP AND

HOW TO SELECT BOOTS AND PACKS FOR LONG-RANGE FOOT MOVEMENTS.

I watched helplessly as the moon continued its inevitable descent toward the horizon while standing on a wind-swept ridgeline in a remote mountain range. It was midnight. My legs and lungs ached, I was carrying too much weight, and in about 30 minutes what little illumination I had was going to vanish. We still had miles and miles to go. Awesome.

Jason and I had been on the move since 4 p.m. as participants of the 24-hour Sniper Adventure Challenge (SAC). This competition combined long-range shooting with extreme fitness, a combination difficult to find anywhere else and yet so vital for those who train for combat.

Shooting competitions usually consist of a whole lot of shooting and nothing more. I like to think of these matches as all sex and no foreplay. They're a lot of fun and can be instructive, but they often fail to address the crucial supporting skills required to survive when we're shooting our guns in a real fight. Combat requires us to be fit because combat requires us to not only shoot, but shoot and move. Fitness matters in combat.

BY Tom Beckstrand

PUT 'EM DOWN

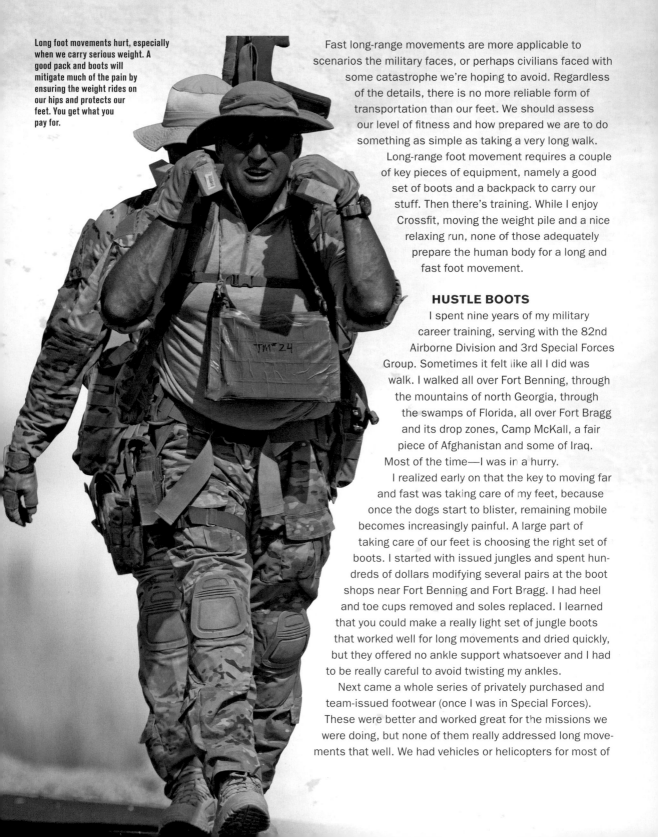

Long foot movements hurt, especially when we carry serious weight. A good pack and boots will mitigate much of the pain by ensuring the weight rides on our hips and protects our feet. You get what you pay for.

Fast long-range movements are more applicable to scenarios the military faces, or perhaps civilians faced with some catastrophe we're hoping to avoid. Regardless of the details, there is no more reliable form of transportation than our feet. We should assess our level of fitness and how prepared we are to do something as simple as taking a very long walk.

Long-range foot movement requires a couple of key pieces of equipment, namely a good set of boots and a backpack to carry our stuff. Then there's training. While I enjoy Crossfit, moving the weight pile and a nice relaxing run, none of those adequately prepare the human body for a long and fast foot movement.

HUSTLE BOOTS

I spent nine years of my military career training, serving with the 82nd Airborne Division and 3rd Special Forces Group. Sometimes it felt like all I did was walk. I walked all over Fort Benning, through the mountains of north Georgia, through the swamps of Florida, all over Fort Bragg and its drop zones, Camp McKall, a fair piece of Afghanistan and some of Iraq. Most of the time—I was in a hurry.

I realized early on that the key to moving far and fast was taking care of my feet, because once the dogs start to blister, remaining mobile becomes increasingly painful. A large part of taking care of our feet is choosing the right set of boots. I started with issued jungles and spent hundreds of dollars modifying several pairs at the boot shops near Fort Benning and Fort Bragg. I had heel and toe cups removed and soles replaced. I learned that you could make a really light set of jungle boots that worked well for long movements and dried quickly, but they offered no ankle support whatsoever and I had to be really careful to avoid twisting my ankles.

Next came a whole series of privately purchased and team-issued footwear (once I was in Special Forces). These were better and worked great for the missions we were doing, but none of them really addressed long movements that well. We had vehicles or helicopters for most of our missions, so this wasn't a huge concern.

I went through Merrell's and didn't find what I needed. Danner has some great boots (I love the Acadias and Pronghorns), but they didn't make anything foot-movement specific at the time. Vasque was good but also lacked something that was movement specific. Then one day I stumbled onto the Lowa Desert Seeker (now updated and called the Desert Uplander). Perfect. "Perfect" is a strong word, so before I go further, let me explain.

The biggest mistake I see people make is buying boots with Gore-Tex liners. I love Gore-Tex, especially if we're standing around in wet or cold weather or doing short movements. It insulates well and is waterproof. Feet have to be kept dry to prevent blisters, so sometimes Gore-Tex is in our best interest. However, Gore-Tex is a horrible idea for boots we'll wear while moving far and fast. While Gore-Tex does breathe, it doesn't breathe fast enough to keep up with even moderate amounts of foot perspiration that come with physical exertion. A good object lesson that demonstrates just how inappropriate Gore-Tex can be for movement is to throw on a set of Gore-Tex rain gear and go for a four- to five-mile run. (Be careful not to overheat if you actually try this.) By the end of the run you'll be close to heat exhaustion. This is what happens to our feet when we wear Gore-Tex boots while doing long movements. Gore-Tex can also encourage blisters

Lowa's Desert Uplander (seen above) does well when we want to move fast. The phenomenal ankle support also helped on those crawls up the mountain.

because it traps so much moisture and keeps our feet soaked in sweat.

Wet, sweat-soaked feet blister easily, so if we do have Gore-Tex boots we can avoid some of the effects by changing our socks often. However, the moisture trapped in the boot will take a long time to evaporate, no matter how many times we change our socks. What we can't avoid is the additional heat Gore-Tex traps causing our feet to get hot and uncomfortable. The point is: avoid Gore-Tex on long movements.

The second mistake I see people make—and have even made myself—is buying boots with thick, rigid soles. These are usually lugged and made by Vibram. You know the type. It's important to tailor sole selection of our boots to the mission the boots will fill, like we would choose barrel contours of our rifles depending on how we are going to use that rifle and under what circumstances.

Thick, rigid soles are great for moving while carrying a heavy load or while moving over extremely rough and broken terrain. The thick, rigid sole works well here because it keeps our foot from flexing excessively, preventing it from beating itself to death inside the boot and from moving around inside, causing blisters. The downside of boots with thick soles is that they're heavy. While 3½ to 4 pounds doesn't sound like much, when we put that weight on the end of our legs and then pick it up and put it down for 20 to 40 miles, the weight becomes exhausting and we feel every ounce.

Thin soles come with problems, too. Thin soles flex more than the

thick ones, so if we're on rough terrain we have a greater probability of blisters. However, if we're moving on trails or along ridgelines where the terrain is mostly flat or a smooth slope, a thin sole isn't a liability.

A thinner sole also places our heels closer to the ground. This is a critical point to consider when shopping for boots in which we will do a lot of walking. The closer our heel is to the ground, the less likely we are to twist our ankle.

Time for another object lesson: Next time Momma gets all dolled up for a night on the town and puts on her high heels, walk behind her and watch how much her ankles roll. Her ankles roll because her heels are so far off the ground that her nice flat and stable feet are now almost vertical and very unstable. Lower is always better and more stable, whether we're talking about shooting positions or heels on boots. We become unstable and stress our ankles when the heel is higher.

A natural response is "I don't have ankle problems." Neither do I. Our goal is to avoid ankle issues, and the closer we keep our heels to the ground, the easier walking will be. Keep in mind that we're probably going to be carrying additional weight on our back and trying to move quickly. The extra weight and quick movement will be their own sources of stress on our ankles and legs.

Lowa's Desert Uplander incorporates all of the principles listed above into one boot and tips the scales at a paltry two pounds per pair. I call my Uplanders my "hustle boots." The Desert Uplander has no Gore-Tex liner and a thinner sole that offers significant weight savings yet is rigid enough to provide adequate support. These boots also keep my heels very close to the ground and offer great ankle support.

I used my Desert Uplanders for my train-up and for the 24-hour SAC. After spending a few months in these boots, I think they're perfect for this task. They're not cheap, nor will they make you a big hit in town, but they're exactly what my feet needed when I was trying to cover a lot of ground quickly. If you're looking to do the same, try them out.

Kifaru's Pointman has the best suspension system. It's light and has no excessive weight or material anywhere. The ruck is also big enough to carry everything for several days outdoors.

YOUR HEATER

Rucksacks (often called backpacks) are the other critical component we need for long-range foot movement. Our ruck is where we'll carry all of the equipment and supplies we'll need for the mission at hand.

A common mistake made with rucks is choosing a flimsy, internal-frame ruck or a frameless ruck for loads exceeding 35 to 45 pounds. Frameless rucks are OK if we're carrying less than 35 pounds

The comp required overland movement for long distances that tested land-nav skills. Weight added up quickly, especially when moving with lots of water.

for less than five hours. Internal frames work well for loads up to 60 pounds and can be carried extensively if we have a quality internal frame, substantially less so for a low-quality internal frame. The only loads I've carried in excess of 60 pounds were always with an external-frame ruck, so I can't speak to the viability of using internal frames at those weights.

The problem with judging rucksacks is that it's hard to quantify the abuse that a bad one gives out because they won't usually leave blisters. A poorly fitted or manufactured rucksack will let us know that it's had enough by either falling apart or placing all of its weight on our shoulders.

When a ruck puts its weight on our shoulders, two things happen and both of them are bad. The first and most noticeable is discomfort.

Weight on our shoulders quickly becomes painful and is the single greatest contributor to helping Special Forces and Ranger candidates quit. Few things are more soul-crushing than the ever-present pain generated by placing weight on a man's shoulders for hours at a time, especially when all we have to do to make the pain go away is sit down.

The second side effect of weight on our shoulders is swelling and numbness in our hands. These symptoms appear more rapidly when it's hot outside and our body is already struggling to cool itself, so fluid collects even more rapidly in our hands, causing swelling and discomfort. It's also why I recommend removing rings and

watches before doing any serious movement.

In cold months the swelling in our hands, when coupled with dehydration and loss of elasticity in our skin, can cause the skin around our fingernails to split. This is incredibly painful and makes even tying our boots a challenge. In either case, swollen and numb hands are an inconvenience and make every task requiring dexterity a chore. This becomes a source of psychological stress.

In my search for quality rucks, I eventually found my way to Kifaru. Kifaru has a reputation for sparing no expense in their effort to craft extremely durable, efficient and comfortable rucksacks. After a conversation with the people at Kifaru, I chose to train and compete with their Pointman.

The Pointman was the right choice for the SAC and any other time I need to carry 60 pounds or less for an indeterminate period of time. It is exceptionally light for such a durable pack, and it tips the scales at a svelte five pounds. I still like this pack after several months of hard use because it has no excess material or weight anywhere and it shows no signs of wear.

The frame system is minimalist, yet offers incredible support while weighing very little. There are two thick aluminum strips that run along the back of the ruck and connect the hip belt to the top of the shoulder straps. The frame is easily sized to ensure that it places no weight on the shoulders, and there isn't a scrap of padding or material anywhere it isn't needed. For those who obsess about carrying excess weight (and we all should), the Pointman is a superb choice for a ruck.

The feature I like the most about the Pointman is its hip belt. Padding is not what makes a ruck comfortable. How effectively a ruck places the weight on our hips and removes it from our shoulders is what determines our comfort level. The hip belt is thin and stiff and, when adjusted properly, places the entire weight of the pack right on the hips where it should be. When coupled with the two aluminum strips that make its frame, the Pointman is exceptionally comfortable, even when worn for 24 hours.

TRAINING

Training for a long-range foot movement consists of doing one thing: walking with weight on our back. No other activity will adequately prepare us for foot movement like foot movement itself. Yes, Crossfit is great, as is weight lifting. Cardio exercise is always a good idea, especially a nice long run.

However, there is no substitute exercise for walking. The muscles we use for walking are very specific and only get a workout when we walk. Walking works the lower legs vigorously, specifically the shins, when we walk fast. The hip flexors also get put to work alongside our quads and glutes.

I recommend walking faster and with heavier weight than we intend on carrying during our exercise. The faster we move, the more quickly we'll fatigue our muscles and, more important, the more our feet will move around in our boots. This conditions our feet and allows them to build calluses where they're needed. It's vital that we condition our feet in the train-up phase or else they'll blister when we walk for real. It's easy to think there's something wrong if our feet need calluses to protect them from our boots. Calluses are essential protection for our feet if we expect to walk 20 to 40 miles at one time. Calluses are how our feet sync to our boots.

My training schedule for the 24-hour SAC had me walking six to 10 miles twice a week with 60 pounds on my back at anywhere from 14 to 17 minutes per mile with a couple of runs thrown in for good measure. I have a nice paved trail near my house with each quarter-mile marked that makes it possible to keep accurate splits and measure distance truthfully. We do ourselves no favors by fudging distance and time to help our self-esteem. In retrospect, this train-up made me competitive for the competition. It wasn't enough to set me up for a win (there were some physical specimens present, and fitness carried the day), but it prepared me for an honorable showing.

TIME AND MONEY

Preparing for long-distance movement requires some money up front for good boots and a good ruck. The two I picked certainly aren't cheap, but I learned early in my career at Ranger School that there wasn't any amount of money I wouldn't spend to make the misery go away once it started. If you spend time walking outdoors for whatever reason, do yourself a favor and get a good pack and good boots. It makes life so much more pleasant.

More important than money is time. Preparing for and executing long-range movements require time under the ruck. There is no substitute. A good schedule is one ruck a week as sustainment and two a week when we enter our train-up phase. As we age, we need to watch for injury, as tendons can easily become inflamed from overuse. I'm pushing 40 and was right on the edge of overuse injury at my "two rucks and two runs a week" schedule. Then again, I'm no fitness freak.

PART III
FEATURES

CAUSE

EFFECT

&

LONG-RANGE SHOOTING
IS ALL ABOUT PROBLEM
SOLVING.

BY TODD HODNETT

Long-range shooting is really a huge math problem with an abundance of variables. There are so many that sometimes we may miss calculating for one or more of them. Depending on the weight of value of the missed variable, this may result in a miss or just a small deviation in point-of-impact shift from where you were aiming. In this chapter, we will talk through a lot of variables, weigh their effect and learn how to isolate the problem and fix it.

Let's first talk about gun setup. There are a lot of issues I see on the range every day at my company, Accuracy 1st. Here are a few.

1. I see a lot of guns that have loose rings, bases or actions, and as the gun is shot, you can see fliers or just larger groups from this. It's easy to fix.

2. I see bipod legs that have the cant locked down too tight. You should be able to move your rifle and adjust for cant with slight pressure, but when you remove your pressure, the gun should stay exactly where you left it for cant. Too many people apply pressure to adjust for level and then hold that pressure because the cant tension adjustment is too tight. This can cause you to completely miss the target at range. We want to be a Ransom Rest for the rifle system to perform off of. We want to remove ourselves from the shot as much as possible.

While we are on the topic of bipods, let's talk about loading bipods for shooting. I teach that to have the best chance of recreating consistency, load the bipods. Some go too far and even end up breaking them. If you are shooting at close range and want to load your bipod into straps on your shooting mat or a steady, rigid object in front of your rifle, this is fine, as it will allow for better recoil management and give you the ability

to watch your own impact. Therefore, you'll be able to adjust quickly in a second-shot correction method. Seeing your own bullet impact is a huge benefit.

However, there are a lot of problems that can occur from this technique when you get out to range. Remember that consistency behind the gun is everything to consistent results. We can't always have the same surface for our bipod legs and may not be able to get the same amount of loading. This may be manageable and not create problems in the short-distance shots. The benefit of extra recoil management may be worth the deviation you may see at short ranges. When we talk long range, the amount of pressure on the bipod legs from shot to shot can greatly increase your group size. Therefore, what I teach is to load the bipod legs with your shoulder to the point that the bipod legs start to roll forward. Then we hold the pressure we have and take the shot. This allows for the shot-to-shot consistency that is required for accuracy at long range.

3. Scope usage is the next issue. I'll start with parallax. This is one of the most misunderstood adjustments with a scope. It seems easy, but it's misused so many times. The ocular adjustment is used to make the reticle crisp. Then we adjust the side parallax, or what I call the target focus. Once both are crisp, we need to make sure

the firearm is stable, then move our head up and down slightly to see if the reticle and the point of aim separate as we move our head. If they do, we have parallax still in the scope. Because some shooters have excellent eyesight, it is hard for them to see a blurred reticle no matter where the ocular is set because their eye is changing shape that quickly. So adjust both while continuing to move your head until there is no separation between the reticle and the point of aim.

If you don't remove all the parallax, you may actually be aiming the reticle where you want the bullet to hit, but the actual point of impact will be somewhere totally different. One way I have found to mitigate this is to set up the rifle so that you see a slight amount of scope shadow (I do mean slight). Having this slight scope shadow ensures that your eye is placed in the center of the scope, thus removing the errors in aiming that can occur from having parallax in your scope and not correcting for it. I shoot every shot like this.

Also, the numbers that represent ranges on the parallax knob are not necessarily correct. In my observation of many different types of scopes, very few range numbers have been correct. I have asked the scope companies about this, and they admit that the numbers are just close. One should never use

Lean forward into the stock of the rifle with your shoulder.

Load your bipod.

these numbers for ranging or to set their parallax range to the same as the range of the shot. This may be close if you are lucky, but one should always adjust the parallax until the target is in focus.

Another potential problem is not knowing whether your scope tracks correctly. Holding is always more accurate than dialing. A friend with a doctorate in optics agrees with me on this. Quality reticles are CNC laser etched. In testing, the turret has been proven not to track perfectly all the time. If you have a scope that does track, it will continue to track, but the key is knowing whether your scope tracks in the first place. I have seen too many that do not track. Remember that, when you test, you want to test at least a 10-mil movement of the scope. One-mil box drills are not testing.

Another issue is having the reticle level for every shot. This is a must. Remember that you will get .05 mil every 100 meters for a scope that is canted 2½ degrees. This means at 5 degrees of cant, you will see around .1 mil every 100 meters. That's a 25-inch miss at 800 meters. This is one of the biggest reasons people miss.

When you make small corrections while zeroing your rifle, the turret may not be accounting for every click. The spring may have loading on it, and the first time you dial the turret, you may get more than you dialed, and it may not go

Twisting a scope's ocular adjusts for reticle crispness.

Think of parallax adjustment as target focus. Ignore numbered "range" markings, as they are usually incorrect for sharp target resolution.

Canting the rifle is one of the easiest ways to miss. Use a level.

Small errors in wind-speed estimation and incorrectly guessing atmospherics will have a profound effect on our ability to hit what we're aiming at. Kestrel's weather meter is an indespensible tool that eliminates these types of errors.

you could double the amount of coriolis that might be in play. This will make you chase your true and not have confidence. Also, make sure you have your ballistic engine accounting for coriolis at all times while in the field.

Be sure to plug in the correct wind direction and speed. This is important in full-crosswind shots, as the aerodynamic jump can result in a higher POI with winds from the right and a lower POI with winds from the left. If this variable is not accounted for, it can also cause an errant true. When you shoot in high winds as much as we do, this could be as much as a 6- to 8-inch POI shift at 600 meters. The Applied Ballistic solver accounts for this effect; most ballistic engines do not.

6. Next up is knowing your rifle. Was that a cold-bore shift or a clean-barrel shift? I was working with a group, truing for one of them at 1,000. I made a wind call for him, and his bullet impacted 2 inches to the right. I apologized for the errant call and started to give him his correction. He stated that it was a good wind call, to which I replied that it couldn't have been good if he got that result. He said that the POI was his cold-bore shift. I asked where his next round would hit, and he was correct in his assessment of halfway to the target from the previous shot. I watched him shoot half-MOA at a grand. I asked him if that was a cold-bore shift or clean. He asked what I meant. I asked him, If he didn't clean the gun after the day of training, where would the CB shot impact? He thought it would still be in the group, so we didn't clean the gun that night. His first shot of the morning was back where his original POI was with a clean-bore impact. I told him he had a stress issue in his gun, and as his barrel heated up, it would relax and shoot nice groups.

Having the knowledge of where your gun hits with a clean bore and with a dirty bore, as well as how many rounds it takes to get back and where those rounds are going, is necessary information.

7. Wind is always the main variable when we miss shots. Having the cor-

back to zero.

4. Next is the overall gun-to-shooter setup. I see guys trying to shoot a gun that is too long for them, and this creates a poor shooting position from which a shooter can't spot his impact. Length of pull, in the traditional sense that we think about LOP, is not meant for rifle shooting. It works perfectly for shotguns, but we don't stand and shoot offhand with our precision rifles. (Some may, but that's not what we are talking about here.)

5. Let's talk about the ballistic side. I point out to my students every week that, when truing a gun, there are several rules that need to be followed. The target needs to be within 20 percent of transonic range. If that range was 800 meters, for example, you would not want to true the ballistic engine under 640 meters. The closer you shoot to trans is optimal for gathering that clean algorithm. Never true more than 20 percent away from transonic range. This will be close to 1,340 fps remaining velocity.

Remember that truing is scientific. I feel that one must true the algorithm

because we cannot accurately account for muzzle velocity to the level we need for long-range precision with most chronographs. If we had a calibrated chrono and actual averaged BCs, we wouldn't need to true. Also, there are too many other variables that this will correct in the algorithm if you are slightly off. One of these is the BC that is suggested by the manufacturer, which may be correct or slightly off, but truing will fix this point as well. Slight miscalculations in bore height can be corrected for. I am not saying that, if you throw a lot of errors into the ballistic engine, truing will fix all of them, but I show in my class that most of the common errors, if the algorithm is trued, will be around .05 mil off the actual impact. This is the thickness of your crosshair.

Another rule is that the range is a known; never mil the target for truing or you can incorporate all your mil-ing errors into your whole range card. Be careful using laser rangefinders and taking the first range you get. Bracket the target, and be sure.

Be sure to plug in the Direction of Fire. If you miss this step while truing, rect cosine for the wind is one variable that is missed a lot. Every clock position off of full is 30 degrees, and we need to account for the 30 minutes of the clock to gain correct wind holds. If you shoot in slight winds and at big targets, you may not see the need. What may show as a 3-inch shift at 600 meters will be more than 12 inches at 600 meters in a 20-mph wind with a miscalculation in a 50 percent value from 1:30 or the correct 71 percent value from 1:30. This is a 4-mph difference.

Let's discuss where the wind is gathered. What I mean is that lying on the ground and looking at the Kestrel may not be the best place to gather the actual wind. Stand up, and face the back of the Kestrel directly into the wind. This will be much more accurate. If you are around terrain features, such as where I train, you have to be aware of orographic and katabatic effects and the probability of gathering accurate readings at your location due to these influences.

8. Now we get into problems we may not cause but have to manage. Trying to manage these combinations of issues along with errors that we add on will compound the issues and result in a low hit probability. I enlisted the use of the Applied Ballistic (WEZ) program to show you the hit probability from a result of these influences. All tables are based on a .300 Win. Mag. firing a 190-grain Sierra MatchKing at 2,700 fps.

The diagrams below show variables limiting effective range.

HIT PROBABILITY DIAGRAMS
(BASED ON .300 WM FIRING A 190-GRAIN SIERRA MATCHKING AT 2,700 FPS)

HIT PROBABILITY BASED ON ACCURACY OF RIFLE/LOAD

Hit probability shown with half-MOA, 1-MOA and 1½-MOA rifle/load combo (15 fps SD for MV, Kestrel used to measure atmospherics, no wind error, 800-meter range).

Half-MOA **1 MOA** **1½-MOA**

HOW STANDARD DEVIATION AFFECTS RANGE

Hit probability shown with standard deviation effects at 800, 1,200 and 1,600 meters (Kestrel used to measure atmospherics, no wind error, assuming 15 fps SD for MV and 1-MOA extreme spread).

800 Meters **1,200 Meters** **1,600 Meters**

HOW WIND-CALLING AFFECTS HIT PROBABILITY

A Kestrel was used to measure atmospherics. Wind error varied. Fifteen fps SD for MV and 1-MOA extreme spread were assumed. Target range is 1,200 meters. A pure crosswind from the 9:00 position was assumed.

+/- 0-MPH Error **+/- 1 MPH Error** **+/- 2 MPH Error**

HOW DENSITY ALTITUDE (TEMP) AFFECTS HIT PROBABILITY

Twenty to 40 degrees or so for temp. A Kestrel was used to measure atmospherics. There was no wind error. Fifteen fps SD for MV and a 1-MOA extreme spread were assumed. Range is 1,200 meters. The temperature was measured to within +/- 3, 5 and 10 degrees.

+/- 3-Degree Error **+/- 5-Degree Error** **+/- 10-Degree Error**

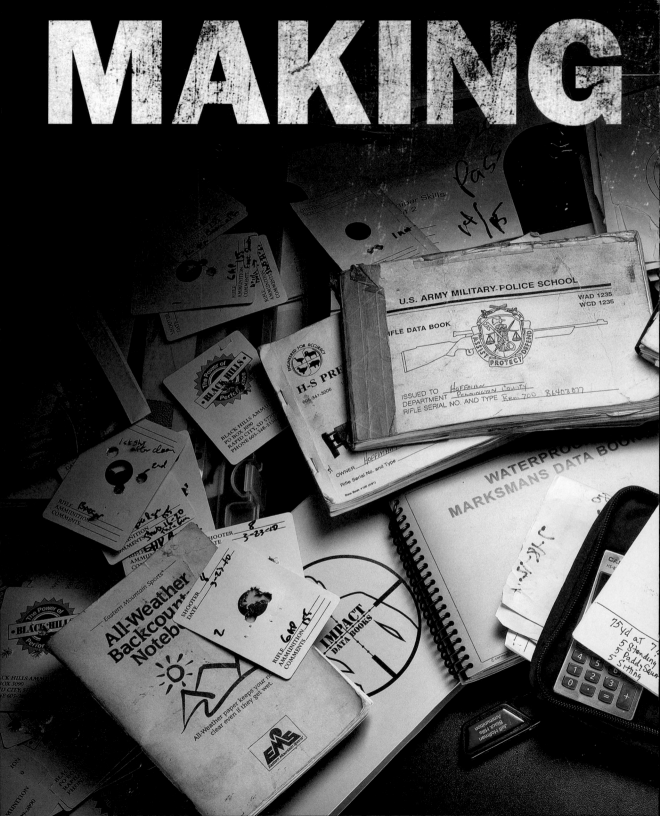

MAKING

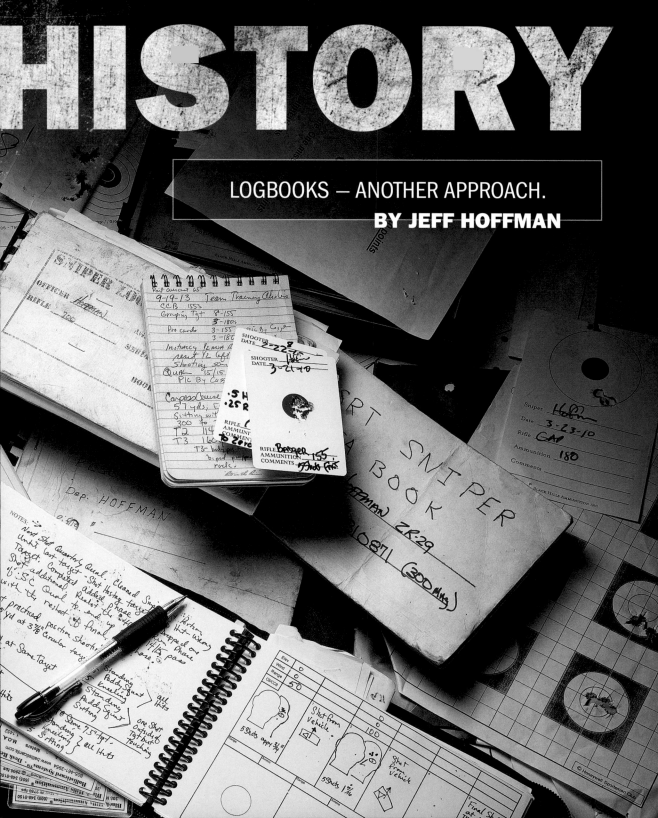

HISTORY

LOGBOOKS — ANOTHER APPROACH.

BY JEFF HOFFMAN

At every basic sniper school, aspiring young snipers are introduced to the logbook. They are taught that it is the key to successful shooting and an absolute requirement for any hope of a successful defense against civil suits that they are cautioned are guaranteed to occur if they are called upon to "Make the shot."

There are many different styles of logbooks, mostly with preprinted targets, and you are taught to meticulously diagram every shot with great detail so the result is a professional document that will stand up in court if needed. You are to log conditions with the instruction that the book will allow you to determine the correct dope for the shot at the time you are called upon to make the shot and save a life. The idea is that you can use the logbook as a reference to find a similar circumstance with weather, range, etc., so you know what adjustments to dial in and save the day in your current situation. You are instructed to fill in the book on the line so that the exact conditions are recorded, and it would have the added benefit of slowing you down during training, to make you a more deliberate shooter. You attach little battery-operated calculators for determining distance with mil formulas and wind effect using the military formula (the one you later learn no one uses because it is too complicated; seriously, who can divide by 13 under stress?). You attach a small flashlight to your logbook so you can read it in the dark. You have a cool camo Cordura cover to hold it all together, along with your ruler and template.

That is the theory. It works, for a while. You diligently log every shot

(well, most of them), plus all light, weather and wind conditions, as well as the date, time, total rounds fired and location. You even follow the rules and try to log every call, in addition to the shot. That detail falls by the wayside quickly, despite the sniper instructors' admonitions. You'll eventually find that you have occasionally made general entries, leaving details on individual shots to fill in later due to the pace of shooting, and you have a little catch-up work to do once you get back from a range session. Therefore, you spend hours at your desk or kitchen table with pencils, templates and a ruler or calipers meticulously building a beautiful logbook with carefully plotted shots and groups measured to the third point after the decimal. If you are a truly dedicated sniper, after a couple of years you have a bundle of great-looking logbooks.

I did this. My team leaders expected it, and after I became a team leader, I expected it. The reality is that it became a chore, and almost every sniper has recollections of trying to reconstruct a logbook after several months of neglect. They would hope that during that time frame, their team leader would not demand to review their book or, heaven forbid, they would have to shoot someone and then be asked to turn over their

logbook to the investigation team, all while knowing the book was incomplete at that moment because they had been busy with other things.

The next phase is that you start increasingly summarizing the training rather than detailing each shot, including your POA, your call and your actual POI. Generally, this phase starts when you are trying to catch up on the book and decide to save time. Then you realize, *Hey, that worked!* and you saved a ton of time, but you still keep trying to maintain a detailed log because that is what you were trained to do.

If you are interested and open-minded, let me tell you what I have learned in 25 years of working with logbooks.

HOW THEY REALLY WORK

Logbooks are unnecessary weight in the field. You already take all the gear you are comfortable carrying. You do not need the extra weight of a logbook on a mission. A competent and experienced sniper would not think of wasting time looking through his logbook hoping to find a similar situation. He would be operating tactically. This is not the time to look up book solutions. The sniper needs to know his firearm, know his dope and be trained well enough to establish the range, wind and lead; get into a position; and make the shot. The window of opportunity is too short to spend time screwing around trying to see how you did this in training. Let me be a bit more clear: If I had a sniper on my team who felt he needed to consult his logbook before he could determine the dope necessary to take a shot, he would quickly be looking for another job. A competent sniper will never rely on a logbook to make a real-life shot; the window of opportunity doesn't allow it. When it is time to perform, you had better be ready to do what you have been trained to do.

I do understand the need for range cards so that you and your spotter agree on target reference points and ranges and can communicate effectively. You can do that with a notebook. You do not need a heavy, bulky, Cordura-covered logbook with a calculator, template and your last eight months of training records with you to accomplish a range card.

Let's address the issue of documentation. I can tell you what I do and what I expect of our team's snipers after 25 years of evolving through the logbook issue. I use a Rite in the Rain notebook and record all pertinent details of that day's training, such as date, range, conditions and round count and an overall round count on the rifle. I record a summary of the training, including distances shot and type of shooting (timed, stress fire, movers, positions, target type, etc.). I record an assessment of my capability that day (half-MOA, three-quarters-MOA, etc.), elevation and windage necessary at the various yardages, and adjustments I made to my zero. What I do not do any longer is draw diagrams showing placement of each individual shot. I do not record my calls unless I called a flier at the moment of the shot. In short, I summarize the training rather than try to record each shot. The difference in time to keep up the book is huge. I no longer have stacks of targets waiting to be entered into an incomplete logbook.

I agree it is necessary to document your training and capabilities, and the logbook is one method of doing so. It is good to document training. Courts have held that, unless training is documented, in the eyes of the court it did not occur. The key thing to recognize is that the logbook is supplemental to other training reports. It does not have to stand alone. Over time, a sniper builds a history of performance and capability with training records from individual training, qualification records, sniper schools attended and possibly awards received, either in department or peer recognition of your efforts, plus perhaps records of attendance and performance at sniper competitions. In our team, we have training plans that are submitted prior to team trainings, and we have post-training reports that document what we actu-

Though logbooks are great for documenting training, a sniper should not take the time to consult one during a critical situation.

ally accomplished in training. We also shoot a group with each of the two ammunition types that we carry (open air and barrier) and send in the groups with our training report. This simple procedure tells command that:

1. We are training.
2. We all have a good zero on our guns.
3. We can all still shoot decent groups.

Over time, the photos we send in build a pretty solid record of our abilities. All this combines to form a picture demonstrating that we are adequately training. This accomplishes the requirement to document sniper training without relying on a logbook in an attempt to record every shot fired for our training history. The logbook is an aid, and you should avoid ever indicating that it is a perfect document accurately recording the existence and details of every shot you ever made. That is an actual impossibility, and that type of position will easily be disproven and leave you looking foolish.

As a rookie police officer, you are taught to write concise reports that cover the facts. Think of the logbook as another arrest report. Cover the facts, but don't waste otherwise productive time. By summarizing your range training, your logbook will be continuously up to date, actually more accurate and less prone to challenge, and you will save a ton of time that is better spent either shooting on the range or with your family, despite what you may have been taught in your basic sniper school.

Tiny, little groups are what every agency likes to document.

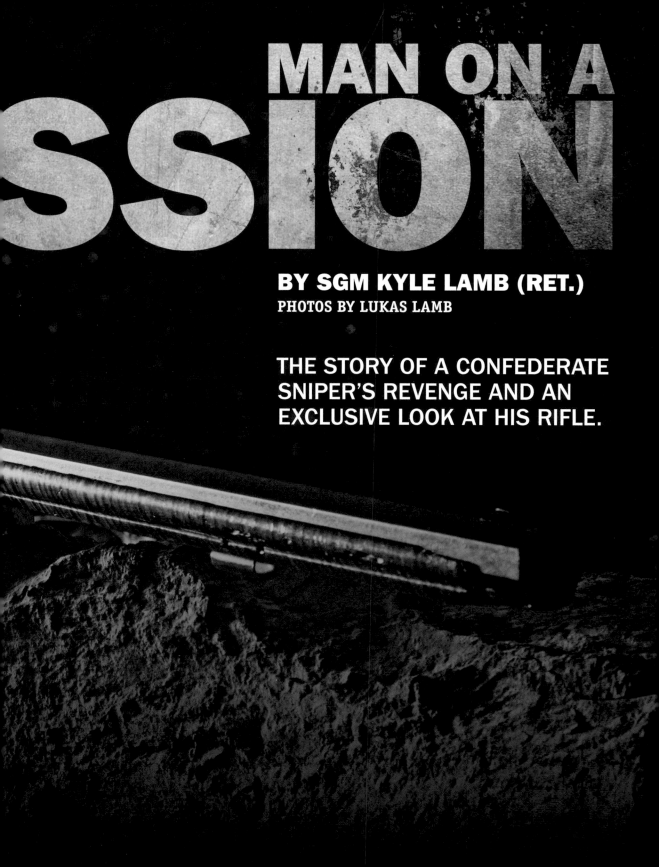

MAN ON A MISSION

BY SGM KYLE LAMB (RET.)
PHOTOS BY LUKAS LAMB

THE STORY OF A CONFEDERATE
SNIPER'S REVENGE AND AN
EXCLUSIVE LOOK AT HIS RIFLE.

Throughout history, man has had the responsibility to do two things: protect his family and provide for that family. In this day and age, some have steered away from their manly roots, but many of us still want to do right by our loved ones. Anyone who considers himself a red-blooded protector of his family will feel his blood boil when he hears the saga of Captain John "Jack" Hinson.

I was running a shotgun class in New York for a group of LE officers, one of whom was also a Civil War reenactor named Dan Phelps. It turns out that he portrays a Southern artilleryman when reenacting battles and has a keen understanding of what the South endured during the U.S. Civil War.

Dan was excited to tell me a few stories about the area in Tennessee to which I recently moved. A few weeks after class, he sent me a book by Lt. Col. Tom McKenney, USMC, Ret., titled *Jack Hinson's One Man War, A Civil War Sniper*. From the moment I read the dustcover, I couldn't put down the book. I was intrigued that the story had taken place within an hour of where I live, but more than that, the story McKenney weaves is really well written and puts you right in the boots of Hinson as he settles the score.

HOW IT STARTED

Jack Hinson lived in a region rife with Civil War battles, the area we now call Land Between the Lakes. In his day, it was simply known as 'Tween the Rivers. It was the section of high ground separating the Cumberland and Tennessee rivers. This area was especially inviting to the Federal Army, for a variety of reasons. Foremost, Johnsonville was a great place to store supplies that could be quickly shuttled upriver to Union forces fighting in southern Tennessee, as well as Georgia. Another interesting fact is that the river flowed north. This

had tactical importance with regard to disabled boats of the gun, troop or supply type, which would float north, back into friendly Union territory.

After several semi-decisive battles in this area, the Union Army set up shop and began patrolling the area to help convince the locals that they might want to stand with the Union rather than fall with the Confederates. Many residents felt the devastation of Union forces on their crops, supplies, servants and homesteads. With supplies running short, Union soldiers and their leaders took what they needed in the name of their cause. This not only included supplies, but labor as well. Many black freedmen, as well as those slaves who had not been granted their freedom, were

enslaved by Union forces in this area for cheap labor.

Enter Jack Hinson. Two of his sons joined the Confederate Army, yet he tried to stay cordial to both sides. Understanding his decision is difficult for us looking through the lens of history, but he was a tobacco farmer who had freed his slaves, all of whom stayed on to work with him on his farm, and he obviously felt that he had a need to stay neutral. Perhaps he truly had not picked the Confederate cause to support.

This all changed one day when two of his other sons headed to the woods to hunt near the Hinson family farm, Bubbling Springs. The Hinson property lay near Dover, Tennessee. The sons were arrested by a Union patrol,

Jack Hinson exacted his revenge in an area of northern Tennessee now called Land Between the Lakes. In his day, the area was referred to as 'Tween the Rivers.

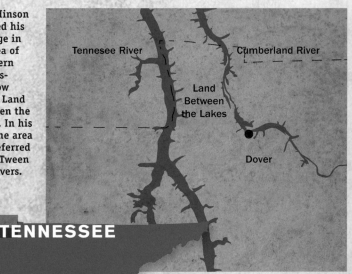

Tennesee River

Cumberland River

Land Between the Lakes

Dover

TENNESSEE

"They murdered my boys, and may yet kill me; but the marks on the barrel of my gun will show that I am a long way ahead in the game now, and am not done yet."

CAPTAIN JOHN "JACK" HINSON
(FROM THE JOURNAL OF B.L. RIDLE, LIEUT.
GENERAL A.P. STEWART'S STAFF C.S.A.)

accused of being bushwhackers and executed on the spot. Their bodies were taken into Dover. Their remains were dragged around the courthouse square, and then, as a further insult, their heads were cut off and placed in a burlap sack. The patrol then rode to Jack's farm and placed the heads of his executed sons on the gateposts of his fence. The soldiers searched Jack's home and surrounding barns from top to bottom looking for contraband, which in this case would be guns. Luckily, they were well hidden.

Jack Hinson picked a side. He swore to himself that he would invoke the law of vengeance for the death and mutilation of his two boys.

ARMING

Captain Jack's first order of business was to acquire a .50-caliber, heavy-barreled rifle. The gun would be of the percussion-cap variety and completely subdued except for the German silver bead on the front sight that would be overlaid on many a Union target. This Kentucky rifle sported a 41-inch rifled barrel that would help him to reach out to nearly a half-mile for his debt settlement with the unsuspecting Union enemy. Jack would be able to load Minie balls for added accuracy, as well as enhanced terminal performance. The Minie ball trumped the round lead ball for performance all the way around. These conical lead bullets became extremely popular during the Civil War, and they continue to dominate today with regard to the blackpowder rifle.

Captain Jack's revenge began as it should, with the elimination of the Lieutenant and Sergeant who were responsible for his sons' beheadings. He knew where their patrols would ride and planned the ambush for

With beautiful wood fitted to an octagonal barrel, Hinson's rifle is in remarkable condition for its age.

weeks. The shots were up close and personal, dropping the Lieutenant from his saddle as he rode past Jack's well-concealed position. Before the smell and smoke from his shot could dissipate into the woods, Jack disappeared like a ghost into his familiar surroundings. Although the Union patrol had the numbers and horses, Jack had surveyed the target area and had a well-planned escape route. On top of this, he was moving in his own backyard. He knew every stone and tree in the woods near his farm. He was able to operate as a true guerilla fighter should. He could hit the enemy at the time and place of his choosing. He took plenty of time to plan his next move.

Shortly after his crusade had started, Old Man Jack became a target himself. It seems he had made the

Union Army's wanted list; they needed to prove a point. The Union hierarchy wanted to show the community what happens when you go against the occupying forces of central Tennessee. In this time and location, many executions took place. Deserters, guerillas, unsupportive locals — no one was immune to the reach of the Union Army. The citizen spies of Dover, Tennessee, launched riders on a wintry night to notify Jack that he would be targeted the next morning by the Union forces. Jack made a decisive move. Disregarding the blizzard that was upon him, he sent his wife and seven of his children west to Sulfur Wells. His two youngest daughters were fighting measles during this chilling trip west to seek safety with relatives. Jack packed up his sniper rifle and headed to the high ground

Hinson's Kentucky rifle sports a 41-inch barrel with an impressive sight radius. Guerrilla-warfare weaponry sure has changed over the last 150 years.

Photos by Lukas Lamb

it through the war, surviving Appomattox, then he walked home, was paroled at Fort Donelson, then died soon after, apparently from malnutrition and exhaustion. Remember that Hinson lost two other sons, beheaded in Dover. Another son had fought as a guerilla in the mid-Tennessee area and was later killed in battle. Last, his two young daughters had succumbed to measles.

Captain Hinson's exploits are the fodder for many fireside sniper stories, but the truth is that he simply did what many of us would do if our family were attacked in such a manner.

The author owes a special thanks to Lt. Col. Tom McKenney, USMC Retired, not only for writing the Jack Hinson story, but for taking the time to help ensure that this article was correct to the best of his knowledge. He also owes Judge Ben Hall McFarlin a debt of gratitude for taking several hours to regale him with stories and allowing SNIPER to photograph the Jack Hinson rifle, which has been passed along to his family. Last, thank you to Fred Prouty from the Tennessee Historical Commission for his help and great stories.

of 'Tween the Rivers. Little did he know that this would be the last time he would see his two little girls, who would succumb to their sickness.

Jack headed to a ridge-top cave that would be his hiding place while he eventually settled the score. From that hiding place, it was an easy climb to a high, angled shooting position that would allow him to prey on Union officers. The Southern Sniper had found the Achilles heel of this Tennessee waterway: Union boats struggling against the rapids, almost coming to a standstill. As though the boats were frozen in time, Jack had plenty of time to steady his rifle and squeeze the trigger after selecting the ranking officer on the Union boat deck.

In the deadly game of sniping, Jack was a master. He not only settled the score, he also continued to cause fear among the Union Army as they braved the woods and waterways of Tennessee. Legend says that the 36 eighth-inch punch marks on his sniper rifle indicate the number of victims who fell to his deadly skill. Others say this was a primitive way of decorating a firearm by local craftsmen. Regardless of which is true, there is no second-guessing his sniping abilities.

Jack was even called to aid Confederate Cavalry leader Nathan Bedford Forrest as a guide for operations in the Land Between the Lakes vicinity.

When all was said and done, this Southern gentleman faded into obscurity. With more than 100 of the enemy eliminated by his sniper expertise, the war had taken a toll on his family as well. Captain Jack Hinson had lost seven children. Two had enlisted as Confederate soldiers, one of whom was wounded, then recovered, only to be killed later in the war, at Petersburg. The other Confederate soldier son made

Photo by Lukas Lamb

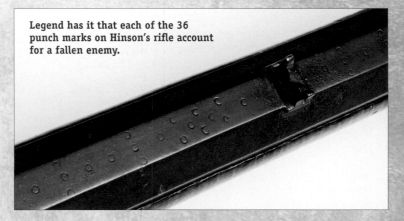

Legend has it that each of the 36 punch marks on Hinson's rifle account for a fallen enemy.

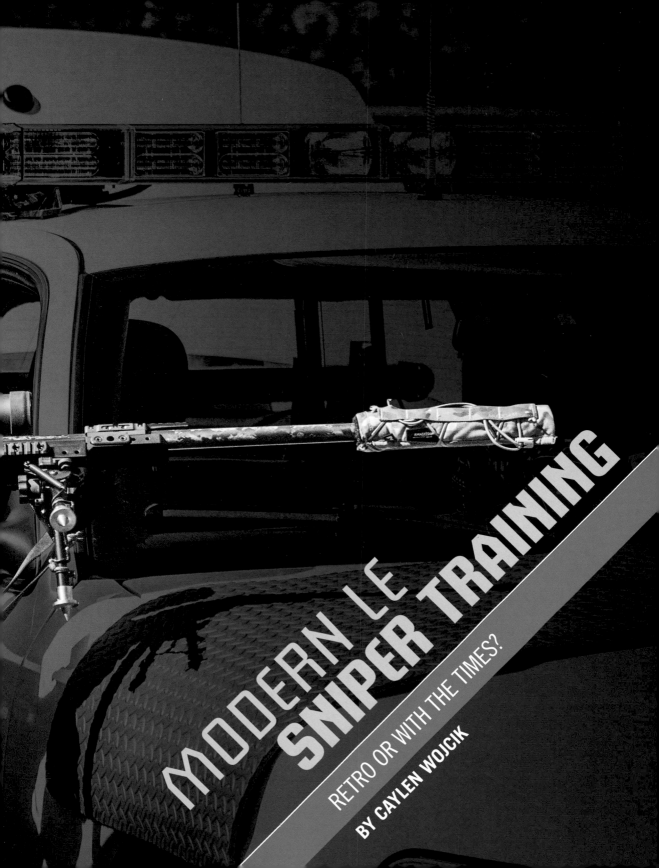

MODERN LE SNIPER TRAINING

RETRO OR WITH THE TIMES?

BY CAYLEN WOJCIK

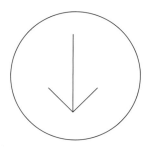

After I give my in-brief to the students of our law enforcement (LE) basic sniper course at Magpul, I begin to go over the topics we'll be covering and the marksmanship qualification. As I describe the qualification course, I see the looks of despair cross the faces of the students when they hear they'll be shooting an eight-part course that includes unconventional positions out to 500 yards and be held to an 80 percent score standard.

Students train for their 150-yard hostage target qualification stage. With a time limit of one minute, students must sprint 50 meters and use the barricades to build any position other than prone, then engage a hostage target with a vital zone roughly the size of a 3x5 card.

The course also covers all the basic skills such as camouflage, collection and reporting of information, observation, urban and vehicle hide construction, and barrier penetration. At the end of every course, I have many students approach me and our staff to tell us that the experience was incredibly eye-opening and that they had never before been exposed to this type of training and shooting.

I used to be astounded by this, but now, after some research, I understand why. The following are my opinions on the deficiencies in LE sniper training. These opinions are based

upon my observations from training military and LE snipers, as well as my own operational experience as a sniper. Before anyone gets wrapped around the axle, this is a topic I care deeply about, and in no way is this article meant to take shots at any particular program. It's an objective look from the outside with the hopes of creating more innovation and novel thinking to form a more effective sniper.

DEPARTMENT TRAINING

I run five-day basic and three-day advanced LE sniper courses in various locations throughout the United States. When we built the curriculum, we looked at many courses and their qualifications as a baseline from which to develop our own. We evaluated everything from content, skills and marksmanship qualification courses. We saw that the bar needed to be raised in a big way. I also spoke with some cadre from established state-sponsored courses and asked questions. The major complaints across the board were the lack of time they were allotted to create a basically trained LE sniper and the equipment with which the students showed up to complete the course. We asked ourselves, What are the absolute necessary skills that a basically trained law enforcement sniper should have when they left our course? Where could we trim the fat?

Let's take a look at the ideal student. The student should have been selected by his team leadership and screened thoroughly for the attributes of a sniper. (What those attributes are fall outside the scope of this article.) Prior to attending any state-sanctioned or privately taught basic sniper course, the student should have undergone a healthy dose of on-the-job training covering all the basics. Before attending a sanctioned course, the student should have a solid understanding of the basics such as the fundamentals of marksmanship, basic angular units of measure, how to build a basic prone shooting position and how to manipulate his optic and firearm. Ensure that the student has had at least one or two runs through your unit's qualification course. Anything less is a disservice to that student.

LE SNIPER SKILLS

1 Law enforcement snipers should be able to move into a final firing position undetected and remain undetected for the duration of the call-out.

2 They should be able to collect and report vital information about the target site and, if required, apply the proper escalation of force and deliver a surgically-placed shot to stop a perceived threat.

3 Barrier penetration and terminal performance.

UNIVERSAL SKILLS

When examining a formal, basic-level school, I expect a student to come away with a solid foundation of core skills from which to build upon. After all, skills are what we look at as tools in the proverbial toolbox. Often, our students will ask for more scenario-based training exercises when they fill out our after-action reports from the course. Should a formal school be responsible for teaching standard operating procedure? All units operate differently, do they not? Perhaps fundamentally they operate the same, but I can't tell you how many discussions I've heard over lunch breaks where students talk about "how we do it at our department," and those tactics can be very different from one unit to another. Leave the building and teaching of standard operating procedures up to the teams that the student is going to spend the most time operating with. The time freed up will allow you to input more skill-building periods of instruction and meaningful practical application into your curriculum.

BASIC VERSUS ADVANCED SKILLS

What denotes a "basic" skill, and what separates that from an "advanced" skill? What should a basically trained law enforcement sniper be capable of? What do we want a sniper to be able to accomplish on a crisis site? A crisis site can be incredibly fluid; you never know what you're going to get. The "what-ifs" are endless, but the fundamentals remain. Law enforcement snipers should be able to move into a final firing position undetected and remain undetected for the duration of the call-out. They should be able to collect and report vital information about the target site and, if required, apply the proper escalation of force and

Students participate in a prolonged stress shoot, which focuses on both target identification and surgical shooting.

MARKSMANSHIP

How do we measure one's ability to be a proficient shooter in a law enforcement sniper application? The current qualification courses for many schools are behind the times. With modern equipment, the FBI sniper qualification isn't difficult (even for a basic shooter), and shooting a B27 from static, sling-supported positions at the 50-yard line or practicing how to low crawl with your rifle across a grass range is a waste of time. Looking at the latest "Police Sniper Utilization Report," there are a wide variety of conditions that law enforcement snipers have been placed in and required to utilize their marksmanship skills. As such, we should be striving to create a marksmanship program to produce a well-rounded and prepared sniper. The program should incorporate cold shots, command fire, surgical shooting under physical and mental duress, unconventional shooting positions, and intermediate-range engagements from practical shooting positions. Exposing students to these varying conditions, and holding them to a high standard while doing it, breeds confidence within the shooter. The chances of most law enforcement snipers making a cranial-vault shot at 450 yards from a tripod-supported standing position are not very high, but if that shooter has the confidence to repeatedly make that shot at 450 yards in a training environment, a 100-yard shot under the same conditions in a real-time crisis becomes reasonable.

An eye-opening experience for the uneducated on the effects of spalling from a 175-grain Sierra MatchKing after penetrating unlaminated glass at a distance of 30 inches.

deliver a surgically-placed shot to stop a perceived threat. The basically trained sniper could immediately be exposed to a very complex situation on a real-deal crisis site. Wouldn't we want that sniper to be as well rounded as possible and confident in his preparedness?

For example, does your basic course cover barrier penetration and terminal performance? I'm not talking about just a lecture but practical application with live fire on commonly found barriers. I sure wouldn't want to be faced with a barrier situation for the first time on a crisis site. This is just one example, but I'm sure you're thinking of several more. Advanced skills are simply the application of the basics under a higher-stress level with more complex problem solving. Trim the fat. If there's something in your curriculum that's applicable perhaps only 10 percent of the time, it's time to deep six that and replace it with something that's going to make your students more confident when they leave your course.

BASIC FIELD SKILLS

Basic field skills such as observation, collecting and reporting of information, camouflage, and techniques of individual movement are absolutely necessary for the student to be exposed to, but we can't expect anyone to be proficient in these areas in 40 to 50 training hours. Nevertheless, we should be approaching this in the same manner as marksmanship: through exposure to the basic, core skills. Is a full-blown military sniper-like stalking exercise applicable? Sure, but these take an immense amount of time, and time is something that many, if not all, programs don't have. Expose the student to the full-meal-deal once, and teach the techniques of individual movement, but after that, focus on ensuring that the student grasps the fundamentals of camouflage and concealment through practical application exercises that are short and to the point. Other skills such as observation, target detection and urban and vehicle hide construction should all be approached the same way. Does the sniper student need to plan and execute a full profile movement into an urban area, construct a hide and collect and report information during a training exercise at a formal school? If there's plenty of time allocated, absolutely. More than likely, though, trying to execute that event inside the constraints of a weeklong basic course isn't going to be very effective. Save the full-profile events for team training outside of the school, and you'll have more time to focus on core skills that the sniper can take back to his unit to more effectively integrate into his team's scheme of maneuver.

DISCONNECT

I believe that there is a distinct gap in communication between the military and law enforcement sniper community. However, I believe this gap is closing and that the law enforcement community can greatly benefit from this cross-pollination. The two disciplines are not as far off from one another as some argue. In combat, I've experienced rules of engagement that have gone from free-for-all to restricted hostile act/hostile intent in a matter of hours. Military snipers do understand escalation of force, and they have valuable operational experience to pass on to our law enforcement counterparts. In extremis hostage rescue, open-air assault, sniper-initiated assaults and supporting noncombatant evacuation operations are all taught at military urban sniper courses, and several of those missions have been performed routinely by military snipers. Institutional inertia is truly what keeps that gap in place, and it must be permanently bridged to secure the flow of information. How do we keep that gap bridged? That lies in the hands of leadership within the SWAT community

to seek out the knowledge. Not everything is going to cross over, but what makes sense should be evaluated through training and, if it's applicable, be placed into the SOP manual.

Rounding this out, it's my feeling that a training program should be a constant progression, and in order to do that, leadership must take a hard look at what's applicable and what's not as well as do some creative thinking. Often that takes someone to look at a program from the outside with the ultimate goal of offering good, constructive criticism. This is a necessary evil, or stagnancy will ultimately prevail and the final product is what suffers. As instructors, we owe it to our students to give them the absolute best training possible and prepare them to confidently execute their duties under a wide variety of circumstances. Their success is a reflection of your success. Anything less is failure, and in this line of work, failure isn't an option.

A Magpul CORE instructor demonstrates the double kneeling position while employing a tripod for support.

BEGINNERS

A COWBOY'S APPROACH TO BALLISTIC SOLVERS.

BY TODD HODNETT

I have been shooting pretty much all my life. At 47 years old, I've racked up just over 40 years of experience shooting long guns. That experience has been peppered with failures to achieve goals that I set, but with those failures has also come the knowledge of where my best-laid plans and efforts went awry.

As I was growing up in the Texas panhandle, guns were a natural part of my life. I lived 20 miles out in the country and had a prairie dog town close by, so target practice was a daily sport. Without a formal shooting background, I thought serious knowledge of ballistics was way over my head.

Experience has taught me otherwise. Ballistics is really pretty easy to understand with some effort and the use of the proper tools. I tell my students that the ballistic solvers we'll discuss here are probably the greatest tools a long gunner could ever have. However,

they are tools, not crutches. We still must have the ability to perform the task without their use. However, given the opportunity, we should always use this wonderful technology.

DEFINING OUR TERMS

In the past, the only way we could replicate the accuracy of the data from a ballistic solver was to shoot every 100 yards out to our limits and write down our dope. Dope stands for Data On Previous Engagements. We would copy all this information into a data book along with the environmental conditions and anything else we might learn on the range or in the field. This process created a reference for use under similar conditions in the future. The data book was our predictor of bullet impacts when faced with variable ranges, density altitudes and wind holds.

Most people think they don't understand ballistics and that it is over their head. This is why we use ballistic solvers. Let the ballistic solver, with all of its crazy algorithms, do the math for us. All we have to do is understand the basics and plug in the correct parameters.

Here are some of the parameters that we need to know:
- Density altitude
- Bore height
- Bullet weight
- Bullet diameter
- Ballistic coefficient
- Twist rate
- Muzzle velocity
- Zero range

Now for a simplified and quick look at each.

Density altitude (DA) is the amount of drag on the bullet caused by the density of the air. At higher altitudes or as the temperature gets hotter, the amount of drag decreases on the bullet. Most shooters understand this and realize that the drop of their bullet will be less under these conditions. Some never think about the effect of wind being less under these same conditions. We derive our density altitude from a handheld weather station such

as the Kestrel. The Kestrel is an exceptional tool and now has a ballistic solver inside of it.

Bore height (BH) is the distance from center of the bore to center of the scope. This is easy to measure and not critical to get exactly dead on.

Bullet weight (BW) measured in grains is usually found printed on the ammo box.

Ballistic coefficient (BC) is the numeric value we give the bullet based on its efficiency in flight or how well it maintains velocity. This number is usually given to us in a G1 drag-scale number. Depending on which drag scale the ballistic solver is using, we can derive a more correct number.

Twist rates allow the solver to accurately estimate spin drift. Spinning the bullet gives us the gyroscopic stability we need, but it can cause the bullet to drift at longer ranges.

Muzzle velocity is usually gathered from a chronograph, but there are other accurate ways of measuring muzzle velocity.

Last, we need to know the range at which our rifle is zeroed.

GETTING STARTED WITH SOLVERS

Acquiring data by shooting every 100 yards or meters is a method still used by a lot of people. I disagree with this approach, as

Here, a Marine is putting his ballistic PDA and Kestrel weather station to good use. With the effective use of these two tools, it is possible to have all of your rifle's data with any load you choose under any conditions with just a few minutes of work.

The data book is dying. Though it was the best option we had for a number of years, modern technology and real-world experience both decisively demonstrate that ballistic solvers are much more effective and efficient.

The Kestrel portable weather station is crucial for effective measurement of weather conditions. Changes in pressure and temperature both significantly impact the trajectory of the bullet, so it is critical that we measure them accurately.

it allows for too much human error. If the shooter is doing a good job shooting, this can be a very accurate way of establishing one's dope. However, it will require many shots, at some expense, and it will consume a lot of time. Using a ballistic solver, we can get the same data with minimal rounds fired in just a few minutes.

Once our gun is zeroed, we enter all of the requested data into the ballistic solver. Our next move is to start with a target at or just before the bullet goes into transonic flight (say, 800 meters for the 7.62 NATO) and then shoot the suggested elevation drop given by the ballistic solver.

Now we need to true our solver to the rifle we're shooting, which means that we have to make the computer match what we're seeing on the range. We do this by changing the MV to get the desired result. In the Horus Atrag solver, there is a page just for this. Horus was the first to offer this option, and it is a very simple process in the Atrag solver.

The first step is to find how far the bullet drops at the greatest distance we can fire before the projectile goes transonic. For the .308, this is about 800 meters. In our ballistic solver we have the

algorithm the bullet is flying on. Once we match where our rounds actually impact at 800 meters to what the solver is telling us, we have trued our rifle to the solver. We now have the capability to calculate the correct drop at ranges in between and ranges farther out.

It's important to understand that nearly all ballistic solvers are just predictive algorithms. This means they are close mathematical guesses, something a ballistician would call a predictive polynomial curve.

This is what I hate, the word "predictive." To a cowboy, that

The ballistic solver works with any caliber, big or small. Once we enter in our weather conditions, muzzle velocity and ballistic coefficient, it's all science after that.

MYTHBUSTERS

When you hear someone say that his ballistic reticle really works well, understand that it can never work at truly long range. If you did decide to dial to correct your ballistic reticle for DA, your wind hold in the reticle would still be in error.

Ballistic reticles and BDC (Ballistic Drop Compensated turrets) all have the same problem. However, they have their place and work great at limited ranges. Most commonly this is around 500 yards. "One size fits all" doesn't work for ballistics. Even if you match your ballistic reticle to the exact muzzle velocity and BC of

means "just close." I wanted more, and I could see the truth. The truth was where my bullet hit. All I wanted to do was have the solver correct the algorithm to where the bullet actually impacted. Like I tell my students, the bullet doesn't get to vote. When you know the actual drop at range, you will accurately know where it will impact at other ranges when using a true ballistic solver.

The next step is to realize that the BC you plug into the solver from the manufacturer is only a suggested BC. This means that even if you have a calibrated

chronograph and a correct DA, you may still get inaccurate predictions at range.

It's really important to realize that the algorithm doesn't separate enough to see the deviation between suggested and actual BCs at closer ranges. Even if you had an error plugged in under the MV, BC or DA, you would still get a suggested hold that would work at closer ranges.

Even at 400 meters you can be off more than 100 fps and still only miss by about one MOA. This MOA error at 400 meters turns into more than a 30-inch miss at 800 meters.

This is a typical screen shot of a ballistic solver. The three top tables represent our gun's information, atmospheric conditions and target distance and speed. The bottom tables give us our holds for both elevation and wind.

your firearm, you will still have issues with DA if you choose to shoot at long ranges or change elevation and temp.

Let's take a look at the effects of DA on a .308. In the following chart, we'll look at the effects of DA in mil holds.

ALT	2,500 feet		7,500 feet	
TEMP	40	80	40	80
300m	**1.4**	**1.4**	**1.4**	**1.3**
500m	**3.8**	**3.7**	**3.5**	**3.4**
700m	**6.8**	**6.4**	**6.1**	**5.9**
900m	**10.7**	**9.9**	**9.4**	**8.9**

As you can see, this is not a huge jump in altitude or temp, but the effects on the bullet increase as we get farther out in range. There's nearly a two-mil shift at 900 meters with only a 5,000-foot elevation and 40-degree temperature swing. A ballistic reticle without the use of a solver can never identify or compensate for this shift. Remember, this elevation and temperature shift will also significantly impact our wind holds.

SITUATIONAL REALITIES

All ballistic engines aren't created the same. I have tested many, and, as you now understand, they all work pretty well out to short ranges but may have huge deviations at distance. The important fact to remember is that we need to always true the algorithm to be precise.

We start the truing process with knowing our DA (usually taken from a handheld Kestrel weather station). Next we need a correctly calibrated chronograph and the actual BC. If we have these three tools, a good ballistic engine will give you the correct hold without truing, but this rarely happens. This is because the BC listed on the box or posted online is often incorrect. This is the problem with computers—junk in equals junk out.

We need to understand that bullet manufacturers list BCs that may be true at 100 meters, but that is not the most accurate number to plug into a ballistic solver. If you want to find the actual BC of the bullet you are shooting, you can follow these few simple steps.

1. Set up a piece of Sheetrock or a paper target at close to transonic range. With a .308, this can be close to 800 meters.
2. Shoot 20 rounds through a chronograph, and take the average muzzle velocity.
3. Place a spotter in the middle of your group.
4. Go back to your shooting position, and find the difference between where you aimed and where your bullets actually hit.
5. True, or change, the BC in the solver to match the results of what you just shot.

Years ago, while I was doing testing on some new bullets, I asked Ken Oehler about this method. He told me that I was getting the actual (not listed) BC. This is the BC that you should plug into your ballistic solver to find the correct firing solution.

One can argue a lot of points about ballistics, BCs, algorithms, drag curves and ballistic solvers, whether in a handheld device, a reticle or a BDC. Like I always say in my classes, you can't argue with where the bullet hits. The method I described here will get you the information you are looking for. Even though this cowboy approach may seem unorthodox to some, I guarantee that if you follow these instructions, you will get better results from your ballistic solver.

AMMO SELECTION

FOR LAW ENFORCEMENT

TIGHT GROUPS ARE NOT THE ONLY CONSIDERATION WHEN CHOOSING EFFECTIVE SNIPER AMMUNITION.

BY JEFF HOFFMAN

Most snipers currently shoot Match BTHP bullets. They shoot these projectiles because they are supremely accurate, and snipers love to shoot tiny, little groups. Let me be more clear. A sniper's entire existence, his reason for being and his ranking among his peers are based upon his ability to shoot tiny, little groups (at least that is the perception). Administrators take pride in the fact that they have snipers who can shoot this type of group. Snipers take pride in that capability as well. In fact, the one way a sniper can measure his capability every time he trains is his ability to shoot these small groups at 100 yards from a prone position.

This is where I need to risk everything by throwing the bullshit flag on yet another corner post of the sniping world. It does a disservice to a sniper to base his entire worth on his ability to shoot small groups, and it's a disservice to his team to base decisions on such a narrowly focused criterion. Things such as fieldcraft, physical conditioning, lethal-force decision-making,

Black Hills' A-MAX is a great open-air round. Nosler's AccuBond is a solid choice for barriers.

observation and reporting skills are harder to measure compared with measuring group size, so those essential skills are often overlooked in evaluating sniper capabilities.

The obsession with group size has had the unintended effect of unnecessarily limiting the sniper's choices in selecting the best ammunition to do his job. I am referring to the incorrect perception that Match BTHP bullets are the best choice for sniper ammunition because "nothing else is accurate enough." This perception requires the sniper to ignore other aspects of ammunition such as terminal effectiveness, avoidance of overpenetration and performance through barriers, all because of the thought that only a Match BTHP projectile is acceptable for sniping. I guess the philosophy is that, if you might be wrong, it is more comfortable to have company. Unfortunately, wrong choices have

consequences, and we are dealing in an area that literally involves life and death.

If Match BTHP is not optimal, what else out there is better? Snipers need accurate ammunition. They also need ammunition that will be terminally effective because their job is to stop the threat. What is terminal effectiveness? It is ammunition that, upon impact, creates an effective wound cavity in order to make the suspect immediately cease to be a lethal threat. The current standard for a "sniping bullet" is a 168- or 175-grain Match BTHP bullet. Match BTHP projectiles were not designed for terminal performance. The projectile manufacturers have repeatedly stated that fact.

Compared with other designs, Match BTHP performance is inferior for sniping purposes. Gelatin testing shows that those bullets generally penetrate about 6 inches with a narrow wound track before the bullet goes into a yaw (turns side-

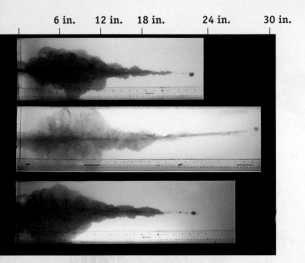

6 in. 12 in. 18 in. 24 in. 30 in.

The AccuBond bullet performs well when fired directly into gelatin and also when fired through glass. In both cases, the bullet begins to perform immediately.

ways) and generally fragments, creating a larger wound channel (temporary cavity). Match BTHP fragments will then continue to around 23 to 29 inches of penetration.

This performance is what generally happens, but even this unacceptable level of performance is not consistent. A penetration depth of 6 inches before bullet performance is excessive, and this only gets worse with range as velocity decreases. There are numerous documented incidents of excessive penetration, insufficient effect on target, and, in one infamous incident, the bullet veered after striking the suspect, exiting and killing the hostage.

When shooting through glass barriers, Match BTHP projectiles also perform poorly. Match BTHP projectiles consistently shed their copper-alloy jacket. The lead core and the jacket then continue as separate, destabilized projectiles. This results in lessened effectiveness on the target; poor accuracy after striking the barrier, resulting in increased risk of mission failure; and collateral damage (shooting people you did not intend to shoot).

What other projectiles offer better performance for the sniper?

OPEN AIR ROUNDS

For an open-air situation (no barriers), snipers need a round that is accu-

GLASS BARRIER ROUNDS FOR SNIPING

Here is the painful truth on the state of sniper preparedness for dealing with glass barriers. Most snipers haven't adequately prepared themselves for the possibility of dealing with glass barriers. It makes their head hurt to think of a problem they don't have a good answer for. Most agencies and snipers have one round only, and that round performs terribly on glass barriers. The agency administration has a multitude of things to deal with that are higher priority than concerning themselves with another type of ammo for a specialized guy in the department. No one is pushing them, so they don't provide the incentive, encouragement and funds to the snipers to solve the problem.

Then there are those snipers who realize there is a problem that needs to be solved, so they have found, and probably purchased on their own, a box of what they feel is appropriate "glass ammo." This ammo is somewhere in their gear for use "in the event that they are faced with a barrier situation." There are several problems here. First is the perception of the need. Note that this category of sniper carries the ammo "in case he is faced with a glass-barrier situation."

Think of this. The reason the team and you, a sniper, have been called to a scene is that a situation exists where a dangerous suspect has been located and is present. That is what a scene is. Since he is still there for you to respond to, that means he is holed up, generally in a building or car. Buildings and cars present glass-barrier problems. I have found that, rather than being "something that might happen," glass-barrier scenes are the norm. You should therefore expect and prepare for them.

The problem is that even if a sniper has thought of this ahead of time and has a box or two of "glass ammo," he is still not prepared. That is like giving a guy a sniper rifle and calling him a sniper. The sniper needs to regularly shoot the ammunition to know exactly where it hits compared with his standard round and confirm his accuracy capability with it. He then needs to do enough shooting through glass barriers so he knows his capability and limitations. He needs to study the different glass barriers that exist in his area and know to what extent he can defeat them with his chosen barrier ammunition.

This is important, because on a callout, you do not want a sniper asking himself what is going to happen if he has to shoot through glass. You want him to look at the situation and know with a degree of certainty and confidence what will happen and whether he can accomplish the shot to save the lives of hostages. I have a rule: "Never ask someone to do in real life anything he has not already done in training."

The truly professional sniper realizes the probability that he will someday be faced with a glass-barrier situation. He has the appropriate ammunition to deal with it. He has trained with it on a regular basis, and he knows the difference in point of impact and can adjust for that if necessary, even under stress. He has trained on glass barriers and documented his training. He is confident in being able to resolve the problem when he is faced with it. This is the sniper you want to be.

rate but also reliably provides consistent, effective on-target performance to stop the threat and limits the possibility of overpenetration of the target to injure a hostage, teammate or citizen in a neighboring home. Examples of this type of projectile would be the Hornady A-MAX or the Tipped MatchKings (TMK) recently developed by the Sierra Bullet Company. This type of ammunition provides consistent results and tremendous effectiveness on target, plus it limits the possibility of overpenetration. Gelatin testing demonstrates that these rounds penetrate no farther than common .40-caliber 180-grain duty loads. The tipped bullets provide better glass-barrier performance than Match BTHP designs. There are also additional projectile designs that are far superior for glass barriers for those situations when you know you are facing a barrier situation.

GLASS ROUNDS

To save a hostage's life by shooting a suspect behind glass barriers, you need to penetrate glass without having jacket separations, and the bullet must then fly true to the target and impact with sufficient mass and velocity to do the job when it gets there. The best projectile choice at this time to accomplish this is a bonded projectile. This means the jacket and core are metallurgically bonded together so the jacket cannot separate from the core when impacting glass. Federal has a bonded round they recommend for glass, and our company, Black Hills Ammunition, has a .308 round utilizing the 180-grain Nosler AccuBond bullet that we have found performs well on glass.

A skilled craftsman can do a better job when he has the right tools. The evolution of sniping has brought us from the past practice of designating a man as the department sniper simply because he was the most avid gun guy and hunter. We now have realistic selection and training standards. We have progressed from the wood-stocked hunting rifle and scope to purpose-built, accurized, synthetic-stocked rifles with specialized optics. It is time we put the same degree of professionalism and care into selecting the right ammunition for the task.

FORMULATING
WIND

I will admit that the number-one reason a rifle shooter misses his target is errant wind calls. I believe wind will always be the nemesis of the long gunner. However, the wind formula should not be the problem. In the past, the wind formulas we used were not fast and required a calculator in the field, unless you were a rocket scientist. People are intimidated by the winds, and they feel like it's a waste of ammunition to shoot on windy days. That's only because they lack confidence. This comes from the fact that there are so many variables we have to account for. There's estimating wind speed and wind direction and factoring ballistic coefficient (BC), muzzle velocity (MV) and density altitude (DA). But it really isn't all that hard.

Let's discuss the problem. In the old long-range shooting manuals we were told that the wind directions gave us a value that we now see as incorrect. Instead of the incorrect method shown below, we now use a more correct and actual mathematical cosine for the angle the wind is blowing against the flight path of our bullet. People argue that they used the old math and it worked. Let me explain why it may have given the shooter a hit and why it was still wrong.

The old depiction of a wind blowing from 1:30 shows a value of half. This makes perfect sense, as the wind from 3 o'clock is full value and 12 o'clock is zero, so halfway between the two should be half value, correct? Not really. The math of a 45-degree is .707 or 70 percent of the actual value of the wind. You can see why if we had a 10-mph wind the real wind value would be seven mph, not five mph. If you are shooting a normal E-type target, which is 19¾ inches by 39½ inches, this small difference in wind value would still result in a hit. But if you tried the old math in a 20-mph wind at 600m and were shooting at a 12-inch plate, the end result would be very different. Your actual hold should be 2.45 mils, and

THE MATH BEHIND YOUR FORMULA SHOULDN'T BE THE HARD PART.

BY Todd Hodnett

This is what was put out in the past and in some areas may be true, but one needs to calibrate to region or specific location.

- ▶ 0-3 mph   Wind can barely be felt
- ▶ 3-5 mph   Wind can be felt on the face and grass may move
- ▶ 5-8 mph   Tree leaves move constant
- ▶ 8-12 mph   Raises dust and loose paper
- ▶ 12-15 mph   Causes small trees to sway
- ▶ 15-20 mph   Causes large trees to sway

Another problem was the actual wind formula being used. I have seen shooters use a generic wind card for a caliber that may not match the MV or BC of their ballistic combination. Also, a lot of wind formulas have constants that are consistently changing, depending on range. These are just Band-Aids that were added to the calculation to try to correct the errors.

LET'S TALK ABOUT A SOLUTION

Now you can be confident in your wind calls. Anyone can do it in his head, with the speed and accuracy of third-grade math-level thinking. It will be correct and custom-made for your gun. And it will be adjusted for density altitude, which we have never addressed before the use of a ballistic computer. If one has been done in the past, it didn't get very far because I have asked every schoolhouse in the military as I travel and no one has seen one, and until the past couple of years, it wasn't accounted for in the wind formulas unless one used a ballistic computer. But now we have a simple answer that corrects for everything.

THIS IS THE WIND FORMULA THAT I CREATED AND HOW TO ADJUST FOR DA

First, take your rifle and find the actual MV either by shooting through a chronograph or by what I do, "truing" the MV in supersonic flight. It is important to "true," in my opinion, because this

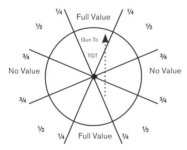

the old way would have given you a wind hold of 1.75 mils. This is a difference in a 14-mph wind call and a 10-mph call. The result is a difference of .7 mils or 16½ inches. Most shooters didn't shoot in high winds, and there are numerous excuses, missing wind-speed estimation being the primary. We don't really know what the wind is doing between the gun and the target. We try to make a best guess in reality, but it is still just that, an educated guess based off movement of vegetation, mirage and Kestrel readings.

Something else we need to discuss is a common misconception about reading wind based off vegetation. The sniper manuals tell us when grass moves and branches sway, but I think it is more important to calibrate our eyes to how much movement the vegetation has in the environment in which we are shooting. I live in a fairly arid region, and the grass, brush and trees do not move as much as they do in many other areas where I find myself training. Therefore, I believe calibrating our eyes to our environment is greatly beneficial for speed and direction of wind. As a pilot, I use the same process as we do as long-range shooters. I am always watching for the wind direction and value. Smoke, wakes on open water, windmills and dust on dirt roads are just a sample of things a pilot may watch for, and if you think about it, all of these can be used by a long-range shooter as well as mirage, vegetation, actual feel and sound. Wind becomes very audible.

will correct for a small error in actual BC from the stated manufacture prediction and what may be actual.

Then use your ballistic computer and remove the spindrift so it doesn't account for it in the firing solution. We do this because we don't want to build a formula for a left-hand or right-hand wind. The result would be slightly different.

Next you plug in the ICO standard for sea level for station pressure, which is 29.92 and a standard temp of 60 degrees and 50 percent humidity. This is done to find the adjustment for DA. I will cover this in a moment.

Now take the first number of your BC and plug that into your computer as a full wind value. For instance, if your BC is .475, you plug in a four-mph wind and depending on your MV, if it is a fast gun or slow (2,650+), you plug in the next whole number lower or higher. Try three mph and four mph from a full-value 3 or 9 o'clock. When I say a fast or slow gun, it really doesn't matter, but you can usually find it faster by using this rule. One could just start at one and two mph, then try three and four mph and so on.

Next look at a target at 500 meters, and we use 500 meters because it is far enough to have a significant wind deflection, but the range is not far enough to give us a large enough variable due to DA.

With 500 meters plugged into your range, observe the wind holds for each mph and pick the one that is closest to .5 mil at 500 meters. This is the same for any rifle and/or BC combination. Now you know what I call your "perfect wind" for that gun.

This allows you to use this number in my Accuracy 1st Quick Wind Formula.

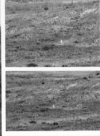

FOUR-MPH WIND BRACKETS (METERS/MILS)

Range	Range Variable	4-7 MPH	8-11 MPH	12-15 MPH	16-19 MPH
100	.1	.1	.2	.3	.4
200	.2	.2	.4	.6	.8
300	.3	.3	.6	.9	1.2
400	.4	.4	.8	1.2	1.6
500	.5	.5	1	1.5	2
600	.7	.7	1.4	2.1	2.8
700	.8	.8	1.6	2.4	3.2
800	.9	.9	1.8	2.7	3.6
900	1	1	2	3	4
1000	1.1	1.1	2.2	3.3	4.4

It's vital we use a wind formula that accounts for the muzzle velocity and BC of our gun. The method discussed here allows us to tailor our wind calculations to our rifle and then generate a wind range card.

NOW LET ME EXPLAIN THE FORMULA.

▶ The formula is RxW+W, or RANGE converted to tenth mils times the multiple of how many times your perfect WIND number will go into the actual wind value, plus the remaining WIND converted to tenth mils.

Say we are shooting a .308 with a MV of 2,600 fps and the BC is .475. This would give us a perfect wind of four mph.

Now we have targets at 400 meters and 500 meters with a wind of 13 mph.

In the first example, you would take .4 for 400 meters and multiply it by three, because 13 divided by four is three with one left over. Up to this point we have only corrected for up to 12 mph since we have a 13-mph wind, and we still have to account for the one mph left over. We now place a decimal in front of the leftover wind and add it to the answer.

EXAMPLES:
▶ 400m w/13-mph wind =
   .4 x 3 + .1 = 1.3 mils

NEXT LET'S DO THE OTHER EXAMPLE
▶ 500m w/13-mph wind =
   .5 x 3 + .1 = 1.6 mils

NOW LET'S TRY DIFFERENT WIND VALUES
▶ 300m w/16-mph wind =
   .3 x 4 = 1.2 mils
▶ 400m w/11-mph wind =
   .4 x 2 + .3 = 1.1 mils
▶ 500m w/10-mph wind =
   .5 x 2.5 or .5 x 2 + .2 =
   1.25 and 1.2 mils

Using half multiples as in the last example is more accurate and is necessary at longer ranges.

LET ME SHOW YOU ANOTHER:
▶ 500m w/15-mph wind =
   5 x 3.5 + .1 = 1.85 mils

Remember that the small errors you may get when rounding are not great enough to result in a miss, as we hope

FOUR-MPH FULL-VALUE WIND

Range	SP 29.9	SP 27.4	SP 24.9	SP 22.4	SP 19.9
200	.19	.18	.16	.14	.12
300	.3	.28	.25	.22	.19
400	.42	.38	.34	.3	.27
500	.56	.5	.44	.39	.34
600	.7	.63	.55	.48	.42
700	.85	.76	.67	.59	.51
800	1.01	.9	.79	.69	.6
900	1.18	1.05	.93	.81	.69
1000	1.36	1.21	1.07	.93	.79

to call wind within one mph, which is our biggest challenge and we are still dealing with the problem of calling the direction of the wind, which will give us more errors than if the math is off. The purpose of this method is to give the shooter the ability to do a wind formula in his head while only using third-grade math and basic multiplication tables. This formula is so easy anyone can do it in his head in a very short manner with accurate results. Simple.

Another variable that will come into play as we shoot farther out is Density Altitude (DA). DA can give us more dense air in which the bullet will deflect farther off the target than it would in the same wind at a higher DA. The way to fix this and have a constant correction is to build a DA table for wind. This is how.

Build a chart that looks like the one below. Take your perfect wind for your gun from a full-value -3 or -9 o'clock, and write down all your wind holds at the different station pressures. I use station pressures of every 2,500 feet, which will give you an accurate enough adjustment and one you can remember. What I don't want to do is build one for every 1,000 feet of DA adjustment and have to look at a chart for winds. You don't have to start at sea level, you can do it for the DA where you are. By starting at sea level you can just build a set of rules that will allow you to always have an adjustment for changing DA.

So, the simple rules for DA for this gun are, sea level and 2,500 feet— after 600 meters +.1 to range value. At 5,000 feet the range value stays un-modified throughout. For 7,500 feet (all ranges) through 10,000 feet up to 600

meters -.1 from range value and then after 600 meters at 10,000 feet -.2. This gives you a custom DA adjustment for your rifle. Even though there may be some small errors at range and at sea level, the shooter would know this and what to do because of building his own personal formula-adjustment table.

DA has a huge effect on how our bullets fly. Most people are aware of the effects on elevation. However, the same effect can be seen from DA with wind. If you take an example of a shot at sea level or 8,000 feet, the difference in a 20-mph wind call is close to a four-inch difference. That is huge. What most people don't understand is that you can get this change in DA without changing elevation. Last year at my house, it was minus 18 degrees and it reached 118 degrees. This is a difference of 9,500 feet in DA. This is a difference in two mils in elevation at 800 meters, but it is a mil difference hold in a 10-mph wind (.308-caliber, 2450 MV, .475 BC).

Wind is always going to be the hardest thing about long-range shooting, but the math behind your formula shouldn't be the hard part. Once you break it down to the fundamentals—wind speed/ cosine/range—there is a good baseline if you just remember to adjust as you feel the wind or direction change.

I had an SF group show up one time, and the wind was howling and it was cold. They told me at the end of that week that they thought I was crazy to think we could shoot 12-inch-size targets out to over 1,000 meters in winds over 30 mph, but now they are mad when they barely miss. "The math is the math," they would say, "and it works."